Vic/Tim

MIKE SIMS

Published by Tate Publishing & Enterprises, LLC
127 E. Trade Center Terrace | Mustang, Oklahoma 73064 USA
1.888.361.9473 | www.tatepublishing.com

Tate Publishing is committed to excellence in the publishing industry. The company reflects the philosophy established by the founders, based on Psalm 68:11,

"The Lord gave the word and great was the company of those who published it."

Cover design by Nino Carlo Suico
Interior design by Manolito Bastasa

Published in the United States of America

ISBN: 978-1-68207-087-1
Family & Relationships / Love & Romance
15.09.02

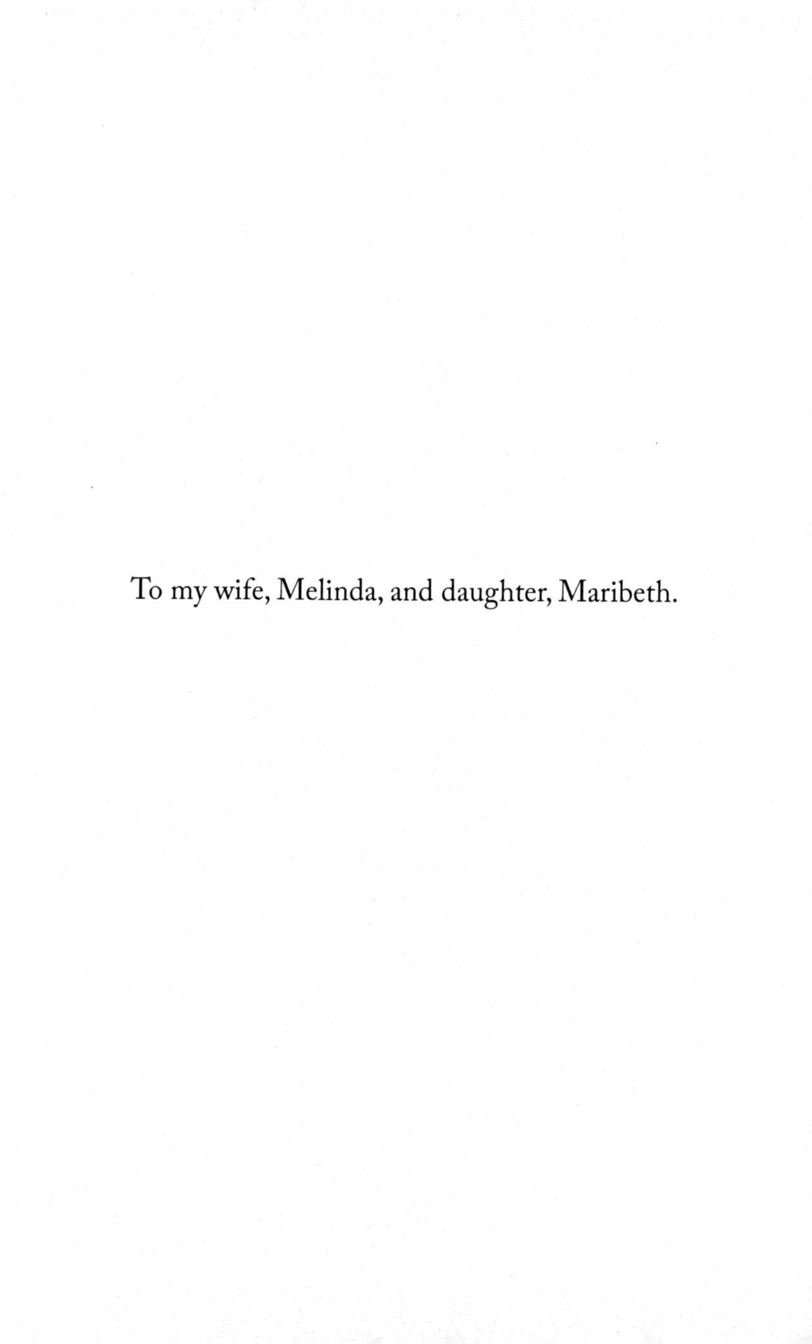

To my wife, Melinda, and daughter, Maribeth.

Acknowledgments

Thank you, Nicole Andani, for your wisdom and support in making this book a reality.

Thank you to everyone who gave their expertise and insight to help make this story.

Contents

The Beginning Encounter

Sometimes what looks like bad people is only good people in bad situations. So what can we say about Vickie Newsome, an advertising executive who is single except for her two cats, Stone and Jones. She named them after one of her first ad sales on a show by the same name. She leaves work as she does most days, not traveling to clients or researching for her job. She plans to make it a quiet evening of watching reruns and wondering what ad could have been put in that show long ago. She makes her way out of her office building and hikes down the street to a local corner grocery to pick up a few things. It is snack night and her night to jump off the diet, if only for a bit. She makes her way back to her car to put her items in the trunk and decides to drop in the bookstore across the street to see what is new. She tends to get lost in these bookstores, so much to discover. She wanders the aisles of self-help books to cooking and to romance novels. A book catches her eye, titled *Short Stories Not from a Real Writer*. The simple book title draws her attention as she picks it up. She is a little aware that someone else has taken notice of her. A mysterious and unseeming suspicious-looking man begins to watch her from corners and small openings in bookshelves. She looks around as if something beckons her to pay attention to her surroundings, but she continues happily looking around. She picks up a few more books and leaves, as it is getting late.

The man follows and gets into his car to continue the pursuit. Vickie arrives at her house in the suburbs remotely, opening her garage door as the man passes by turning the corner. She made a small mental note of him passing. He must live around here, that's why the car seemed to go wherever she went when coming home. She leaves the garage door open as she carries her goods into the house.

The man sees she is inside and sneaks his way into her garage and hides behind a cabinet so she will not notice him. She grabs her final things and closes the trunk of the car as the garage door lowers. As it closes, her security light automatically comes out outside when dark. The man watches as the light extinguishes from the garage door closure. He waits patiently for a long time so that her guard will be down. He listens for the TV in her house to eventually go off. He knows the longer he waits, the more neighbors will go too. Thoughts race through his mind of doubts about what he wants to do. However, the urge is strong and the adrenaline is pumping in his anxious state. It is like a drug, for this is something he had fantasized numerous times in his head, but his emotions have convinced him to make the fantasy real. He is scared yet excited and knows there is no going back after this. It runs through his mind like a car in a circle with no place to park as he keeps hearing her shuffle around her house. Finally, it is getting quiet as he hears her walking up the stairs. He makes his move to the garage house door, noticing it is unlocked. Vickie is showering and preparing for bed. The man has made his way up the stairs and takes position in an adjacent room waiting the right moment for him to surprise his victim.

Vickie dries off after a short shower and changes into a long t-shirt. The man's heart begins to beat faster as the moment has come. He has not done this before but has rehearsed it many times in his head. He is no killer but pulls his steak knife out that he acquired from her kitchen for intimidation. She is sitting on her bed reading now. He thinks to himself, *Okay, Tim, this is it*. He begins to have second thoughts about his life and why he is doing this, but the obsession to control another human being is too much of a high for him. Chemical responses in his brain from the excitement are like a drug and he begins to feel powerful.

He summons his courage and bursts out, quickly overtaking Vickie and putting the knife to her throat. He covers her mouth immediately and tells her not to make a sound. She stares intently at him and down at the knife. Tim tells her to comply with his wishes and she won't get hurt. He then tells her that he is going to take his hand off her and she must take her clothes off. He asks her if she understands as, and she nods slowly yes. He releases her and she slowly stands up to lift her shirt off. She then looks behind Tim and says, "Thank God you are here."

Tim quickly turns to see who is behind him and no one is there. Turning back quickly, he is kicked in the chest hard by Vickie, knocking him against the clothes drawers. By this time, she has grabbed his hand with the knife and turned his wrist, forcing him to drop the knife on the floor. He panics and begins to try to make a break for it as he labors to breathe from the kick. However, she is too quick for him and pushes him against a wall corner. He falls back, stunned.

By the time he gets up, she has a short wooden stick about three feet long and cracks him across the back as he makes it to the stairs. He tumbles, hitting the wall at the bottom. Looking up in horror, she is running down the stairs with a look of fury on her face. He runs to the fireplace and picks up a poker to defend himself, but she has already deflected his thrust and hits him in the arm with the stick, causing him to drop the poker. He is badly hurt, and she cracks him again across the temple of his head. He is dazed and slowly gets up, seeing everything fuzzy. She is standing there hardly out of breath and staring at him like a lion about to finish its kill. He pleads with her to do no more and he will gladly go to jail. Like out of a martial art movie, she spins around and lands her foot across his sternum, knocking him backward again on the ground. His speech is slurred as he quietly begs, "No more, no more," then blacks out.

Tim wakes up and he is sitting on a chair as he looks over and Vickie is sitting in the chair in front of him smoking an e-cigarette. His eyes grow large wondering what is next. He pleads with her to let him go and he has learned his lesson.

Vickie says, "You know, I was a rape victim before when I was a teenager. It nearly destroyed me. I felt suicidal because I thought there was somcthing wrong with me. I had a hard time with relationships with men as I grew up. I went to a lot of therapy and it cost a lot, not just in terms of money, but life. All because a man wanted to have sex with someone other than his own wife. I understand more than you might think about how men tick. Some are weak and have very little control like you. So since the time of my attack long ago, I have earned three black belts and work out regularly. Because I know that it could happen again.

I trained and prepared for the day that someone like you would attack me. I know you perverts are not diminishing in numbers, you are growing. Now you have the internet and easy access to porn and other shock images to tantalize you. But what happens when that is not enough? You guys have to carry it further into the real world. It is like a line that you cross and the line moves further. Blame it on hormones or bad childhood, but the fact is you types have no restraint. You travel further into depths of depravity rationalizing that it is now normal and okay. Before you know, it won't just be rape but murder to get your feelings nurtured. Well, I am going to teach you about being violated. I am going to show you what it is to have your life ruined. You are going to know what it is to be a victim, Timothy. I have copied your driver's license, I know all about you now. Amazing, the same internet that feeds you maniacs can also give me all the information about you that I could possibly want. This will be therapeutic for both of us. Well, more for me. And I know there is nothing you can do because if you try to get me in trouble, your fingerprints, even DNA from your ass whooping, is all over my place, especially the knife you threatened me with. So go now and let us begin this learning experience for you. Go ahead. I said go!"

He stares in horror that he is trapped in a nightmare he can never leave. She has him and he knows his only chance is to comply and maybe she will leave him alone.

Tim gathers up all the strength he can and carries himself out of her house as she stares at him. He looks back and says, "I'm sorry."

Vickie says, "Well, I am sorry too, Tim. See you around."

Tim gulps as he leaves. He walks very slowly and staggers back to this car. He leaves for home.

Escape from Vickie

Tim drives home to his subdivision about forty-five minutes away. He walks up to the door, barely hanging on and rings the doorbell. His wife answers and asks him in horror what happened to him. She helps him inside and his daughter age eight asks her mother, Lana, if daddy is okay. The mother assures her everything is okay and tells her to go back to bed. Once they are alone, Lana asks Tim what happened. She was worried he was so late. Tim says that he had car problems and while he was looking at his car, a gang of kids beat him and took his wallet. Lana responds that they should call the police right away.

Tim says, "No, they know where I live and said if any trouble with the law happens they will come after us. It is best to just leave it be."

Lana says, "I told you about your late evening excursions. I know you need time to yourself, but I wish I knew what you needed. We all have needs, you know. Need to stop peeping tomcatting around."

Tim looks at her with a horrid face as she says, "Sorry, that was mean. I don't mean to make light of this."

Tim nods yes as Lana doctors him and helps him to bed. He lays down and tells Lana, "I love you and I am thankful you are in my life."

Lana smiles. "What would you do without me? For one thing, you need to take better care of yourself. What if something happened to me?"

"I hope not, I need you to keep me out of trouble."

Tim smiles as Lana replies, "I can't do that for you, honey. Besides, it's not like you are likely to get in trouble on purpose." She nurses his wounds as he starts to drift off to sleep. Lana whispers to herself, "What did you get yourself into?"

Back to Work

Tim has taken the rest of the week off to recover. The following Monday, he arrives at work less bruised and in better spirits. He tells a story of how the gang attacked him. His fellow coworkers tell him he is lucky that he only lost his wallet and not his life. Tim is called into his boss's office and he asks him if he is okay otherwise. Tim is surprised and asks why. His boss explains there has been a collection agent calling all week wanting to know your whereabouts because of some debts you owe. Tim explains it must be a mistake because he has no outstanding debts. His boss tells him that he should then deal with this as soon as possible because as he knows a schoolteacher is supposed to set an example at school for his students.

Tim says, "I am sure it is identity theft from the attack I had."

Tim moves to retrieves the days of phone messages left by the collection agent. He looks down and the agent's name is Vickie and the name of the collection company wrote down is "Vic/Tim Time To Pay Inc." He goes to a nearby phone and calls the phone number which comes back as an operator for the victim abuse line for battered and raped women. He hangs up and crams the messages into his pocket. The bell rings for school and he rushes to his class.

Tim storms into his classroom and the class laughs. One of the junior high kids proclaims, "You're late, Mr. Jenkins. Were you out peeping through people's windows?"

Some of the students in the class give a big "Ooooh."

Tim looks up at the student and says, "Why would you ask a silly question like that?"

The student replied, "It is a joke that our guest speaker made about you being gone. She said you must have been out being a peeping Tom."

"That is a not a funny thing to say about a teacher especially in these days, you can't even joke about such things."

"Sorry, Mr. Jenkins. It seemed funny when that Vickie lady said it."

Tim's eyes grew big and he stared for a moment at the student. Then Tim asked, "What guest speaker? When?"

"Yesterday she was here for career day. She talked to us about the advertising business. She used you as an example for the whole hour practically."

"What else did she say, like what examples did she give?"

"She just talked about different types of people, you know. Like normal people and weirdos. Oh, yea, like she said that she had to understand people's issues like rapist and so forth. She said that everyone has little devils that tug at them, begging them to do bad things. Her job is to appeal to the bad in people without driving them over the edge and stuff."

"Well, I don't know how you remember that so well when you can't seem to remember sentence structures."

The student laughs and responds, "Well, if you were a blonde babe like she was then I would remember everything. I wouldn't mind being a peeping Tom for that!"

Tim turns around from the board and assertively responds, "Don't ever talk about peeping Toms or rapist in my class again, understand?"

The student quietly responds back; "Sure thing, Mr. Jenkins. Like I said, I am sorry."

Tim turns around and begins writing on the board and talking about grammar as the students look at each other bewildered and smirking.

First Impressions

Tim leaves school at the end of the day and wanders to his favorite bookstore out of pure habit, as if his brain is on autopilot. He starts combing through the books on literature and a feeling begins to drape over him as he realizes that this is the store he first saw Vickie in. He begins to calmly but briskly leave and sees Vickie outside the bookstore on a patio side cafe table staring at him. He looks around and walks over to her table to sit down.

He says, "Look, you got me good with the beating, and the collection agent thing, and the guest speaker thing. Just leave me be and I will seek help. I beg you to leave me alone now."

Vickie puts down her book and looks at him for a moment then leans forward. "Tim, Tim, I haven't even gotten started yet. Don't you know that? It is over when I say it is and not before." She leans back in her chair with a look of disgust.

Tim looks around, very bothered. "You know what, you are harassing me. That stunt you pulled in school as a guest speaker. Really? I could go to the police, you know."

She smiles at him and reaches into her purse. She pulls out a ziplock bag with the knife Tim left behind at her house he used to threaten her. The bag, marked in black bold letters, says "Exhibit A."

"Go ahead and call the police. Then you can explain how your fingerprints are all over this knife and at my residence too, or don't you remember that? Go back to your life. I have a lot in store for you." She gives a slight smile that seems to cover pain. Tim is horrified, almost in tears as he clumsily gets up to leave but can hardly take his eyes off her, when she says, "Oh, you should read this short stories book. It is pretty funny and sad. You can get a lot out of books you know." Bewildered by her attitude, he leaves.

Tim arrives home and tells his family he is not hungry as he goes upstairs to lie in bed. His wife comes up later and starts to comfort him. She says, "Honey, I know you have been through a lot. More than any person deserves. Try to rest and put it all behind you." She kisses him and tends to their daughter.

He can only stare off into the wall as if the wall is miles away. He is reviewing the whole predicament eyes focusing and defocusing on the ceiling patterns. Tim comes out of the shower and sees blood all over the bed trailing to his daughter's room. He runs frantically as he sees his wife and daughter stabbed to death and the knife he used at Vickie's is still in his wife's chest. He turns and looks to his left and Vickie is there and runs toward him. Suddenly, the alarm clock is buzzing for him to wake up. He gets up and looks over to see his wife sleeping. He walks over to his daughter's room and stares at her sleeping. He always gets up much earlier so he can jog before breakfast, but today he just spends his time looking at his family back and forth till they wake. He finally breaks away and begins to get ready for work, passing by his chair and table and seeing a book laying there, the very same one Vickie was reading outside the bookstore. He picks it up and flips the pages.

"Ah, you got yourself another book, I see. Is it good?" his wife asks.

He turns and says, "Yes, quite." He puts it down and leaves.

Sticky Vickie

It is Tuesday and everything seems uneventful all the way through Friday. He feels good after a good day at school. The class is happy about it being the end of the week. He stops and gets a couple of roses, one for each of the women in his life. He feels that maybe finally Vickie has given up on him.

As he walks in the door to his home, he sees Vickie has his daughter in a headlock. He immediately storms in the living room, demanding to know what she is doing here. Vickie stops to let go of his daughter, Tanya.

Tanya and Tim's wife look back at Tim intently. Lana asks, "What is wrong, dear? Vickie was just showing Tanya how to defend herself against attackers. You know there are a lot of rapists and child abductors in the world."

Tim, confused, asks, "Vickie is teaching her this?"

His wife replies with a smile, "I'm sorry, honey. This is Vickie. She runs a home business on the side teaching self-defense right in your own home. She stopped by a while ago and was giving us some free lessons."

Vickie stands up and holds her hand out to shake Tim's. Vickie says, "Need to work on your grip there, Tim, kind of weak. Bet I could take you in a fight. But, wow, you have a strong parental feeling. I can tell you cherish this little girl of yours. I am sure you want her to know how to defend herself against attackers. Lots of perverts out there, you know, and you don't want her to grow up with memories like that. What do you think, Tim, what should they do to people like that?"

Tim replies, "Maybe punish them, I guess, but some maybe are just sick, you know, in the head."

"You're right, Tim, sick. But even dogs are put down for attacking people and the dog is just under the influence of instinct."

"Well, well, well, yes, but wouldn't a class somewhere be more appropriate?"

"You are absolutely right, Tim. I am an associate martial arts teacher down at Sato's Karate Gym. Here is a card, why don't you come down with your family and I can teach all of you some pointers, for free, of course. My way of saying sorry for this intrusion into your home."

Tim looks around trying to grasp an excuse until his wife says, "Sounds great! We will be there tomorrow night as you suggested earlier."

Tim is speechless as Vickie looks at him and says, "Don't worry about bringing a knife, we have some rubber ones to practice with. You know most home intruders bring a knife because it is quiet, unlike a gun, especially if their intention is to rape. Usually it is robbers that bring a gun because they want to scare a person as much as possible. You got to know these things, Tim, in case someone wants to do harm to you and your family. When you come down tomorrow evening, I will show you exactly what I mean by that."

Tim's heart is racing as the innuendos never cease, it seems. Lana asks Vickie if she has read this short stories book her husband picked up. Lana had read it and found it interesting, telling Vickie that Tim gave her a book on their first date.

Vickie says, "Hmm, that is good to know. I have seen that book by the way. In a way it kind of changed the course of my life. How about you, Tim?"

"I think that book has set a lot in motion."

Vickie smiles and says good-bye to the rest as they warmly say good-bye back. Tim just stands there listening to his wife close the front door. As she passes, she says, "She is a nice lady. Did you know she was attacked twice by rapists? Once as a teenager and another time not long ago. She said she was able to beat the last guy pretty well till he got away. I tell you, I would hate to be on that woman's list. Did you have a good day today, dear?"

Tim snaps out of his semihypnotized state and says, "Fine, yeah fine." He goes to help with dinner.

Journey Interrupted

A NEW DAY and a new dawn. It is Saturday and Tim begins his routine of jogging around the trails. Suddenly Vickie starts jogging next to him.

Tim says, "We won't be going to your martial art class tonight because I am not playing into your game anymore."

"You don't have any choice, Tim. remember exhibit A? Besides, you might actually learn something important. At least do it for your wife and daughter because what I can teach them might save them from a pervert like you someday."

Tim stops and pleads, "Just leave me and my family alone,"

Vickie turns and looks at him. "You just don't get it, do you? You just don't break into my house and try to violate my body and walk away. I could have killed you that night, but…" She looks away tearing up.

"But what?"

Vickie says, "Just be there tonight or wonder what else I will leave in your house for your wife to find." Vickie laughs fakingly and runs off. Tim gets back home to eat breakfast and take a shower.

Defense

Tim and his family run errands and later that evening they arrive at Vickie's martial art school. They enter and sit in the chairs off to the side. Vickie is in customary Japanese Aikido apparel for fighting as she takes on three other top students at Shodan level in the school. They attack her as she plunges the first one straight into the second and then flips the third onto his back. She begins speaking to the other students on the mat, explaining what she just did. Vickie calls for one of the students she just threw to do a certain attack, which she flawlessly defends against, sending the opponent down again.

Tim swallows as his wife looks at him. Lana says, "It is okay, honey? She isn't going to be doing that to you…I hope."

Tim looks at his wife as she smiles and looks back at Vickie, terrified. Vickie catches Tim's look and has an intent look on her face. She calls out of one of her demonstration students again and tells him to come at her with a rubber knife. She then portrays exactly the same attack she had done to Tim at her house on the martial art opponent. She viscously attacks him, hurting him and eventually pinning him down. She apologizes to the student for being too hard. After the class is over, she goes over to Tim and his family to welcome them. She tells them she is going to teach them how to deal with an attacker. Tim is trying to get away but Vickie and his family persuades him to put on padding to protect his groin area and a chest pad. Vickie then hands him a knife and tells him to attack her. Tim is scared but Vickie reassures him that she will go slowly. Tim slowly lunges the knife at her and she kicks him in the groin almost lifting him off the ground. She apologizes and says she sometimes gets carried away but will be easier next time. Tim is in pain and getting mad. He squares off and she flips him to the mat, pinning his arm down that holds the knife.

She looks at him and whispers in his ear, "See, Tim, I could have used a variety of things. You are lucky I used what I did on you. I could have killed you or paralyzed your perverted ass. Who would you rape then?"

Tim jumps up even more mad and squares off. Vickie taunts him, saying, "C'mon, Tim, do it like you mean it."

Tim comes at her fast like he wants to jab the rubber knife right through her. She steps out of the way to let him continue his attack. Lana calls out to Tim to take it easy. Tim is not paying any attention and goes even harder at Vickie. Finally, Vickie grabs his arm over her shoulder, spins to put her back side to him, and drives her hip into him to throw him over her back. He lands a few feet away flat on his back, hurt. Lana and Tanya run over to Tim and help him up.

Lana angrily says, "What the hell were you doing? You just can't get mad and try to attack someone because they embarrassed you. Vickie is a trained expert. She could have killed you if she wanted to!" Lana looks back at Vickie as Tim groans in pain. "Vickie, I am so sorry for this. Could you please excuse us? Tanya and I will be back some other time to take lessons from you but Tim needs to stay home."

Vickie responds, "That is no problem and, Tim, sorry you had to be on the brunt of my defense. Maybe you should work on your emotions and find some inner peace, helped me all these years. But thank you for letting me at least show what to do to would-be rapists." Tim looks back at her with an angry look as his wife and daughter help him out of there.

Sunday rolls around and Tim is resting out in the backyard. His daughter is off to a girl scout meeting and his wife comes out to see if he is okay. Tim just stares at the ground as Lana asks, "What's wrong, Tim? Are you still shook up over yesterday?"

Tim starts to speak softly and stutters, "I have to tell you something."

Lana looks concerned even more. "What, Tim?"

Tim responds like a shy child. "I met Vickie before she came over the other day."

"I know, Tim, she told me. She was quite surprised to have stumbled onto our house when she went door to door. When I mentioned your name she asked if it was you and told me all about you and her."

"Sh-she did?"

"Yes, Tim. She told me how you saw her drop her wallet out of her purse at the bookstore and could not get her attention before she drove off. Then you followed her to her house and caught up with her to give it back. That was the night you were beaten up by the gang on the way home. And that is why you didn't want me to call the police because you were worried about what I would think of you being over there at that time."

"Yes, I didn't want you to get the idea I was up to something."

"It is okay, you are a good man. That is why I married you…I guess. Just kidding. Just relax and enjoy your day."

Tim stares off, feeling like his whole life is being used like a puppet by Vickie. All he can do is play along and hope she cuts the strings soon.

Recipe for Disaster

Tim comes home from Monday's work and has a pleasant dinner with his family. Tanya goes over to a friend's to play as Tim sits down with Lana for a nice evening of talking.

Tim says, "I bought a book today but it is confusing me."

Lana replies, "What book?"

Tim states laughingly, "It is called *Ventriloquism For Dummies* but I don't know which one of us is supposed to read it, me or the dummy?"

Lana replies, "What's the difference?"

Tim's laughter dies down at the retort. Both then laugh heartily as the doorbell rings. Tim's laugh slowly dies down as his wife goes and answers the door. Tim nearly spits out a peanut he has just put in his mouth when he hears his wife say, "Hi, Vickie, come on in."

Vickie and Lana walk into the living room and sit down.

Lana tells Vickie, "Tim was just telling me the funniest joke about him buying the book *Ventriloquism for Dummies* but he does not know which one should read it, him or the dummy."

They both laugh as Tim has a half smile on his face. Vickie says, "That's a good one, Tim, but I am not sure it makes much difference who reads it." Lana laughs with Vickie as Tim just starts fuming. Then Vickie says, "You know, as my main job is an advertising expert, I am trained in some psychology. It is amazing what you can theorize about people even by the jokes they tell."

Lana responds; "Wow, tell me what is bothering Tim?"

Vickie sits up close to Tim and looks him over as if she is reading the sweating pores on his face. She then sits back and says, "I think Tim feels himself to be a puppet in life, kind of like the dummy from his joke. Probably from childhood, he must have been a victim of some trauma. Even though he plays the part of a good parent and citizen, he feels like a puppet to his past or even to a person. He may feel the strings are being run by someone he knows, but really it is from his own mania. An unresolved issue that he feels he privately has to lash out and make others feel the pain inside him. His place of refuge is books. It is there he feels safe."

Tim looks on like a deer in headlights as Lana says, "That is incredible, you are very insightful. You know, for years Tim had to go to counseling even some more after we got married. When he was a child he was abducted and abused by a predator but was later let go. It took a lot for him to get over that. I am impressed by your observations."

Vickie says, "Well, that is just a guess but that is what my job is. You have to really know people in order to sell working ads to them. Lana, tell me, how did you two met?"

"Well, it was quite a coincidence. I was working at a bookstore when Tim came in. We both were just out of college and he was starting his career as a schoolteacher. He was so shy but I kept seeing him looking over at me once in a while. It was so cute. After work I went home to my parents' house and I saw him drive by and waved. He stopped and asked me if I lived there. He said he was trying to get back to the beltway and for some reason tried to cut through this subdivision. I knew then it must be fate. I gave him my number and asked him to please call me. I thought he was going to almost cry. But he called and we went out, he gave me a wonderful book, and we fell in love, so years later here we are."

Vickie says, "That is a beautiful story, Lana. It must have been fate for sure, or he was stalking you, ha-ha."

Lana and Vickie starting laughing and Tim sat there with a pale look on his face. Vickie asks, "How did Timmy there get along with your parents?"

"Oh, my dad hated him, mainly because Dad caught him staring through my window one night. He chased him off and called him a little peeping Tom. But later let him come over. I respected my parents' wishes even though I was an adult. I kind of liked the way he kept coming around."

Vickie laughs and looks at Tim. "You were just a little pervert and I knew you were a peeping Tom just by looking at you."

Tim looks back with his face turning red.

Lana says, "Honey, don't be embarrassed, she is just kidding. I would not have married a pervert."

Lana tells Tim the real reason Vickie is over is because she wanted her to tell him it is okay about him dropping her wallet off.

Vickie says, "That's right, Tim, I appreciate what you did. You never know what a person will do when they have your driver's license. Anyway, Tim, don't worry, you are just stressed. You have a lot to think about since your attack the other week, I am sure. What a strange coincidence that he brings my wallet and loses his. Anyway, I have to leave."

Tim quickly responds, "How did you know I lost my wallet?"

Vickie looks at Lana and back at Tim and says, "Lana told me everything that happened. You need to be careful, lots of identity theft out there. You never know when someone wants to pretend to be someone else." Lana walks her to the door and invites her to dinner during the week. Vickie accepts while Tim sits with his face in his hands.

Lana sits down and asks Tim what is wrong. He says; "I don't want you to hang out with that Vickie woman."

"Why? What is wrong that you don't like Vickie?"

"Look, I think it is just best we stay away from her. I can't explain why but my feeling is she is major trouble. I think she is after one of us and it may not be good. She is single and very aggressive, I am worried."

"My God, you think she is lesbian?"

Tim looks around and says, "Yes, that's it. She is after you. That is why she keeps wanting to do so many things for us."

Lana looks around as well and says, "Well, I don't know. Maybe you are not used to a woman of her type. I invited her for dinner this week, let's just get this out and tell her you are concerned."

Tim very quickly responds, "No! I, mean I am not sure that will work. Can't we just break off contact with her?"

Lana tells him, "You are being irrational. Just let us talk to her, okay? It would be a nice change around here." He looks off and just sits with his thoughts racing.

The days pass slowly for Tim and the night of the dinner visit has finally come. Vickie shows up, stunning in appearance, embarrassing Lana.

Lana tells her, "I did not mean you to get so fancied up for this dinner."

Vickie laughs it off, saying, "It was not my intention to embarrass you, but I just came out of an important meeting at work."

"Oh, okay. Tim, would you pass the corn?" Tim is in a daze staring at Vickie as Vickie blows a kiss at him.

Lana says, "Uh hmm, Tim?"

"What?"

"The corn, honey."

"Oh, yes, here you go. You look very nice, Vickie.

"Why, thank you, Tim. Very gentlemanly of you," Vickie replies.

Lana smiles at Tim as she passes food around.

Vickie asks Tim, "You know, this happens to be what I wore the night you rescued my wallet." Tim starts choking and looks up as he clears his throat.

Lana asks, "Are you all right, honey?"

"I'm fine."

Vickie asks, "So, Tim, how did you manage to get away from those gang kids that robbed you that night?"

Tim just stares at Vickie intently. Lana looks at both and says, "He was very lucky, I think he is still shook up about it. He does not handle stress well."

Tim interrupts, "Lana?"

Lana smiles and continues eating.

Vickie says, "I'm sorry. I did not mean to bring up that painful memory. Sometimes, though, it is better to get things out in the open."

Tim replies, "Okay, maybe you are right. I will talk about that night and just bring it all out. That way we will all know. How does that sound, Vickie?"

Vickie has a smug smile as she stares for a bit at Tim, knowing he really does not want to say anything. But Vickie knows this and lets him squirm at the prospect of her calling his bluff. Vickie then stares down at her food for a moment and says, "Tim, you obviously have a lot to process about your attack. They must have really beaten you down and it must be hard for a grown man to be whipped by someone inferior. Give yourself some time to contemplate it. But you know, someday, it will have to come out. Are you prepared for that?"

Tim is staring knives at Vickie while his fear of her puppetry and threats is moving to anger. Vickie can read his eyes like a book and says, "What are you going to do about it…Tim?" The silence is deafening as the tension of the strings between puppet and puppeteer tighten to almost the breaking point. Lana intercedes just as Tim is about to say something in anger.

"Are you guys ready for dessert? Let me get it and give us a chance to cool off with some nice ice cream and peach cobbler." Lana gets up with a fake smile, hoping that will hold them.

Tim continues to stare at Vickie as she silently says with her lips, "You want to end this? Meet me tomorrow at noon at the bookstore."

Tim calms as a glimmer of hope has just washed over him and shakes his head in a yes motion. Lana comes back with dessert and it is apparent to her that her trick had worked as they all seem calmer now.

Tim sniffs and asks, "You smoke, Vickie?"

"No, Tim, I don't. Why, does that bother you?"

Tim, remembering during his initial encounter with Vickie that she smoked says, "My mistake, you just seemed like a smoker."

"The only time I ever smoked was when I was attacked by a home invader not long ago." Tim's faces drop as silence and staring happens between Vickie and Tim.

Lana says, "It must be me because I burned something I was going to surprise you with, but it did not work out. I'm sorry, Vickie, Tim hates smoking."

"That's okay, Lana, I used to smoke long ago but I quit when…well, that was a long time ago."

Tim looks over at Vickie, noticing a kink in her armor. After eating, Tim states he is going to get their daughter from the babysitter and would be back. Lana asks Vickie to stay and look at some old pictures in their album. Tim would ordinarily be disturbed but knows it does not matter after tomorrow as he proceeds out the door in a better frame of mind.

Exam Day

The next day, he leaves for lunch and meets Vickie at the bookstore. He has been looking forward to this day and starts out telling Vickie, "We have been through a lot, and I want you to know how sorry I am and glad this is ending. I am a better person now and you have changed me, thank you."

Vickie smiles and says, "Sure you are. Take a look, Tim, at that woman over there, the brunette reading the science fiction."

Tim looks over at the lady and says, "What about her?"

Vickie asks; "Do you find her attractive? Does she interest you? She looks like she is in her twenties, got the cute naughty librarian glasses, and not paying attention to her surroundings. Bet she would be easy prey for someone like you."

Tim is visibly embarrassed and nervously asks, "Why are you asking me this? Can we please just end this?"

Vickie replies, "Not by a long shot, mister. First, we need to stalk this girl and see about you taking her like you tried to take me."

Tim, horrified, responds, "Are you serious? I-I-I can't do that?"

"Sure you can and you will because I know you want to. This time I have your back on it so you won't mess up. You are going to do whatever your fantasy desires. Look, she is leaving to buy that book. Let's get in my car and follow her."

Tim follows her but pleads not to do this. Vickie informs him he has no choice as they get in her car. Tim looks down at her console and she has pictures of this girl and her home address as well as other information. Tim asks, "My God, you have been stalking her. All to have me do this? I thought you were disgusted with me as why you were putting me through this and now you want me to rape this girl? What the hell is wrong with you?"

"Yes, I watched her for a few days and I have seen her in there before so I know you have seen her too. Don't lie to me and tell me she has not been on your radar. You are going to do this and I am going to make sure of it."

Tim pleads with her not to go through with this as she starts driving and following the girl. "Look, maybe I can do this another time. I don't feel well and want to go back to work."

Vickie ignores him as she stops near an apartment complex and watches the girl going to the apartment, then states, "Apartment 214, second floor. She keeps an emergency key under a fake rock in the plant next to her front door. Use it to gain entrance when you see her go to her balcony to water the plants there. She does that every time she comes home. Then do your business."

Tim contemplates just running out of the car as Vickie says, "If you run on me, I will run you over."

Tim slowly, nervously opens the door a little and then starts crying saying; "I can't do it! I just can't do it!"

Vickie asks, "Why not?"

Tim replies, "That is our babysitter and she is a nice girl. I taught her a few years ago. I just can't do it! She was my favorite student. Don't you see?" Tim continues to cry.

Vickie says, "Close the door, we are leaving."

Tim closes it and mumbles to himself, "I don't want to live like this, I can't stand it."

Vickie says, "Tim, if you would have took me up on this offer to rape that poor kid, I would have done you in. I wanted you to face this issue with someone I knew you cared about. I knew who that girl was, Lana told me. She also told me how this girl was failing and was about to quit school but you took her under your wing and helped her graduate. Now, when you see all women, I want you to think of her and your daughter, get it?"

Tim looks up at Vickie and says, "I get it."

Not a word is spoken till they arrive back at his car at the bookstore.

"Tim, this is not over with. You and I have a lot of unfinished business together. See you soon."

Tim's sadness turns to horror as he realizes the puppetry continues.

The Darkness Becomes Us

WEEKS PASS WITH no evidence of Vickie around and Tim's life seems to be returning to normal. He has begun to be more proactive in his daughter's life and enjoying himself more.

One day, Tanya asks, "Daddy, I want to go outside and ride my bike."

"Only for thirty minutes. It will be lunch soon and then we got some fun things to do this fine Saturday."

"Thanks, Daddy," Tanya says, and runs out the door.

Tim smiles as if all is right in the world. He goes and sees what his wife is doing lunch-wise and chats with her.

"You know, I feel good. I have not felt this good in a long time."

"That is good, honey, I was getting worried about you. Especially when Vickie is around. You know I like her a lot but for some reason she seems to have it in for you."

"She is okay. She means well. I could live without her though."

They both put the lunch on the table and Lana goes outside to get Tanya. Tim can hear her yelling for Tanya to come in but keeps yelling for her. A bad feeling washes over Tim as he goes outside and sees Tanya's bike sitting on the ground down the sidewalk but no Tanya anywhere. They both start yelling for her but no reply. Immediately they start knocking on neighbors' doors but no one has seen her. The bad feeling turns to fear as it is apparent she is gone. Lana goes into the house and starts calling people, yet no one knows where she is. They call the police and as police and relatives arrive, they begin searching to no avail. No one has seen anything, as if Tanya has vanished into thin air. Police check for anyone having surveillance cameras but no one has any. Neighbors, relatives, friends all drive around trying to find poor Tanya. Every store checked but nothing.

Tim tells his wife, "I will be back."Tim drives to Vickie's house with a growing anger. He is convinced that she has taken his daughter. He pulls up to her house and storms to the front door and pounds the door as if to knock it down.

Vickie answers calmly and says, "What's up, Tim?"

He passes her, entering her house and says, "I want my daughter, you bitch!"

Vickie responds, "Tim, I think you better calm down and tell me what you are talking about."

"You know damn well what I am talking about. You kidnapped Tanya this afternoon. I want her back right now or I swear to God, I will go to the police after I kick your ass."

Vickie responds with concern, "No, Tim, kicking my ass is not possible as I have proven. As for police, there is nothing to go to them with. I do not have your daughter. Are you sure she is not at a friend's playing?"

"No! We have checked with all her friends. She is not there or anywhere."

Realizing that Vickie does not have her, Tim begins to break down, sitting on her couch crying. Vickie sits down next to him.

"Tim, I have no idea what happened to Tanya. Go home and let the police do their job." Vickie walks him back to his car as Tim asks, "You would tell me if you knew anything, wouldn't you?"

Vickie replies, "Of course I would. My issue is with you, not your daughter."

Tim gets in his car and drives around the neighborhood for a while hoping to see Tanya and then goes home. Tim arrives home to his worried crying wife and Tim looks like he is exhausted. Neighbors and relatives help them inside their home and comfort them. Minutes pass like hours and hours like days as nighttime falls with no sign of Tanya.

It is midnight and the phone rings. Tim answers as the voice says, "Mr. Jenkins, this is Sergeant Thomas at the precinct four police station. Detectives have your daughter and she is at our location on Baldwin Street."

Tim cries and asks if she is all right. Sergeant Thomas assures him she is okay, just a little shook up. Tim thanks him and hangs up the phone in relief, telling his wife and everyone the good news. Lana and Tim immediately drive to the station as they meet the sergeant.

Sergeant Thomas says, "She is shook up, as I said on the phone. The detectives have been asking her questions."

Lana asks where they found her.

The sergeant states, "She was found tied to a bed in one of your neighbor's houses two streets down. We got an anonymous tip that she was there. When we arrived, we found the kidnapper dead and had apparently been beaten to death almost unrecognizable. We think whoever did it was the one that called us. Anyway, let me take you to the detectives and your daughter."

He walks them down. Λs thcy scc Tanya, she yells, "Mommy! Daddy!"

They all embrace in tears of joy and relief. The detectives ask Tim if they could talk to him in private for a few moments. Tim says, "Sure. I will be back, honey." Then he kisses Tanya and follows the detectives. They go into an interrogation room as Tim says, "You don't know how thankful I am you guys got her back."

The older Detective Skanks says, "Well, Mr. Jenkins, we are very pleased your daughter is back. We have some questions though about where did you go earlier this afternoon."

Tim's happiness turns to concern when he replies, "I'm not sure what you are referring about. I went to a friend's to see if she had seen Tanya."

Detective Skanks says, "Who is this friend?"

Tim replies "Vickie, Vickie Newsome."

The detectives look at each other and Detective Skanks replies, "And she can corroborate your story?"

Tim replies nervously, "Yes, she can, I hope she can. Why what is this about?"

Detective Skanks says, "It seems a little suspicious that you disappear for a while. We got an anonymous call shortly after and find your daughter in a registered pedophile's house with the pedophile beaten to death. That sounds like maybe you found this pervert, beat him to death but left your daughter there so you would not be tied to the homicide."

Tim is horrified. "No, sir, I did not have anything to do with it. I was at Vickie's. Call her, she will tell you."

The young detective leaves the room while the Detective Skanks just stares at him as if he was guilty as sin. The young detective calls Detective Skanks out of the room for a while. After a few minutes, they return. Detective Skanks says, "Well, Tim, we have a huge problem. Miss Newsome tells us she has not seen you at all. Matter of fact, some of the neighbors saw you driving around the area of the victim's house where he had your daughter. You have anything to tell us?"

Tim says, "Look, I don't know what is going on with Vickie, but I swear I was at her house for a short time and then I went driving around to find my daughter."

Detective Skanks says, "All right, we are going to let you walk so you can be with your daughter. But don't leave town, we will have some more questions for you later."

Tim gets up to leave and the young detective tells him, "You know, I probably would have done the same thing myself if I found the pervert that took my child."

Tim looks back at him and replies, "I did not do anything."

The young detective responds sarcastically, "Right."

Tim rejoins his wife and daughter as they leave the station and drives back home to a resounding reunion of family and friends.

I Am Not She

The next day, Tim and Lana wake up with Tanya sleeping between them. They turn on the TV as the news is vibrantly reporting about the kidnapping and homicide of the kidnapper. Police state they have a person of interest but no real leads on the killer. Tim gets up to dress and goes outside to get the Sunday paper as neighbors are outside looking at him whispering amongst themselves.

His neighbor John walks over and shakes his hand. "Damn good what you did, Tim."

Puzzled, Tim asks, "What?"

"You know what. I would have done the same to that son of a bitch pervert. Everyone knows you did it. Police have been up and down all morning asking questions about you. Anyway, I just want you to know I am behind what you did."

John gives him the thumbs up and winks as he walks back to his lawn mowing. Tim looks around in horror as he realizes that everyone is looking at him like a killer. He slowly looks around at the disturbed faces of his friends and neighbors and walks back into the house. He goes back into the bedroom where Lana is playing with Tanya's hair as she sleeps like the sleep of angels. Lana sees the dismay on Tim's face and asks what is wrong.

Tim says, "I did not tell you but last night the police questioned me as if I was the one who killed that kidnapper. I am apparently the person of interest the news is talking about. And John just told me he liked what he thinks I did. All the other neighbors think I am a killer."

Lana responds, "That is ridiculous, you don't have a mean bone in your body. I know you are not capable of that."

Tim looks around thinking about the bad things he has done or attempted to do to Vickie. Lana looks at Tanya as her face changes and asks, "Tim, you really did not do anything to that guy, did you?"

Tim replies in disgust, "How can you ask that of me?"

"I'm sorry, but I don't think anyone would blame you if you found our daughter and confronted that pedophile. You probably had no choice but to fight him, even if you surprised him. I think any father would have done him in."

"I know, but I really did not do it. I don't know what I would have done if I had found him. I am not as sure of myself as someone like Vickie—" Tim pauses and mumbles, "Vickie."

Lana says, "Honey, are you all right?"

Tim says, "I will be back. I will bring back some food."

Tim leaves and drives over to Vickie's house. He hesitates as he is about to knock on the door and Vickie opens it and say; "Welcome, Tim, I knew you would be back."

Tim walks in and sits on the couch. Vickie is sitting in a robe reading a book looking up at Tim then asks, "So, what brings you back so soon?"

Tim stares at her for a while till she finally puts the book down and gives him her full attention. Tim asks, "Why haven't you asked me about my daughter."

Vickie says, "Oh, yeah, did you ever find her?"

"You know we did. You found her, didn't you? That kidnapper was beaten so badly they almost could not identify him. Someone powerful took him out, someone like you. You did it, didn't you?"

Vickie smiles. "Yes. I looked on the registered sex offender database and found three in your neighborhood. I had watched your house and saw this guy in his car days before staring at your daughter. So after your visit last night, I went looking at those three sex offender's houses and saw one had the car of the guy I saw watching your daughter that time. I went to his house and he answered the door. He tried to get rid of me, but I forced my way in and heard the whimpering sounds of a young girl in the bedroom. I immediately opened the door and saw Tanya blindfolded and tied to the bed. At that point, the kidnapper grabbed me and I broke his arm and then his knee. I got a baseball bat he had and beat him from feet to arms, then from hip to chest. I made him pay for what he was going to do to Tanya. Then I drove away and called the police from a payphone to let them know where Tanya was." Vickie sat with a smug look on her face of extreme satisfaction.

Tim, looking like a ghost, replies, "Now the police think I did it, especially when you told them I never saw you that evening."

Vickie laughed. "Of course I put this on you. No one would blame you for what they think you did. If they caught you in one lie they knew you did it and would look no further. The fact is, since there is no evidence you were there, you won't get convicted."

"I did not do it is the issue. I am being blamed for something I did not do."

Vickie's face turned serious and replies, "But what about the things the police don't know you really did, like try to rape me. You got away with that and now you want justice? You can't always expect good things to happen when you have done bad. It is the trap that life sets up. Think you better just go home and think about it."

Realizing he is guilty of some things and not others, throws Tim into a severe state of depression and confusion. He gets up to leave as Vickie tells him, "You know, Timmy, there is a thing called 'karma' and it just may come visiting you this weekend." Tim stares back tearful as he leaves.

Scout's Honor

After a few weeks, things seem to have quieted down for Tim and his family. However, many of his neighbors avoided them as they were not sure if he killed the kidnapper or not. Police have gone cold on the case, having no relevant evidence tying him to the crime itself. It seems for now the issue is over. Vickie has been quiet all this time with no communication. But Tim knows it is a matter of time before she shows up again. But he thinks maybe she will eventually lose interest and let him live his life. That is until Tanya says, "Daddy, guess what?"

"What, kiddo?"

"Miss Vickie is my new scout troop leader!" Tanya exclaims.

Tim tries to keep a smile on his face as he knows he has just moved into another scenario with Vickie. He responds, "That's great! What does she have planned for you girls?"

"She is going to teach us self-defense. She said she will make sure nothing happens to me like when the bad man got me. She is so strong, I don't fear things when I am around her."

Tanya smiles and runs back to her room as Tim grows disgusted and angry. He goes in the kitchen and asks his wife if she knew about Vickie troop leading their daughter. Lana responds, "Yes, Tim, she had talked about it for a while but they are very careful about who they let volunteer with these kids. I think it is the best thing for our daughter. Tanya finally wants to go and do things now she knows Vickie is there to watch her."

"I know she would defend our daughter with her life, but I just don't know if it is a good idea."

"And why not? What is it with you about Vickie? She has done nothing but been nice to us and help us out. I think you are still upset about being beaten up by those gang kids because you helped her and that she is a strong woman. Now since the kidnapping incident you just seem to blame her for that too."

"I don't blame her for the kidnapping."

"Well, you sure seem to blame her for something. You just seem to be more and more uneasy since then. As for Vickie watching Tanya, I feel perfectly safe with that and that says a lot since I almost lost my daughter recently."

"*Our* daughter, you mean."

"Yes, our daughter is what I meant."

Lana is visibly upset as Tim looks at her and says, "You blame me for Tanya being kidnapped, don't you?"

Lana stares at the sink and looks up to say, "Now you are interrogating me like the police did you? You want to know how I feel? I'm hurt because I feel like there is a part of you I don't know. Maybe it is the kidnapper being killed and no one seems to know who did it. Maybe because you can't explain where you were that day. Maybe it is the weird obsession you have with Vickie. I just feel there is something hidden inside you I never knew existed and you won't share it with me. To be honest, I am scared and hurt. Yes, I feel like you are at fault for our daughter getting kidnapped even though I know it was not your fault. I'm sorry, it's just a little hard for me right now. I just need to get away for a while. I am thinking when Tanya goes to camp for the week, I want to stay at my mom's that week. Clear my head."

Tim, astonished, watches Lana walk off crying to the bedroom. He sits down and stares at the TV screen even though it is not on. Everything Lana said and the events of the recent past just spin in his head like a race car on a track. His eye looks past the TV to the outside window behind it and his eyes focus on the car parked in front of his house. It is the detectives staring at his house and they drive off. He begins to get more depressed as he thinks about it.

Head Wrapping

The next day during his lunchtime, he makes a call to a psychiatrist for an appointment. She agrees to see him and he visits her office the next day. His psychiatrist, Tammy Stines, cordially greets him.

"Welcome to my office, Tim. May I call you that? Please call me Tammy."

"Thank you, Tammy."

"Tim, I know about you and the whole kidnapping issue, I saw it on the news. I recognized your name right off when you made the appointment. Obviously you are here because of these events, right?"

"Wow, you are good. Yes, that is part. The other part is I am having issues with my wife because of it and having an issue with another woman as well."

"Oh, I see. Tim, I have helped a lot of guys caught in extramarital affairs—"

Tim quickly replies, "No, no not an affair. Just, well, this other woman is a problem."

"Well, okay, I am one for two. I am your therapist so start by telling me what is on your mind."

Tim takes a breath and says, "This woman's name is Vickie and I found a wallet she dropped and returned it to her house and after that I was, um, beaten up by gang kids on the way home. But after that, Vickie seemed to get involved in every aspect of my life. She stalks me and even now is my daughter's scout troop leader. She is—"

Tim is suddenly cut off by Tammy, who says, "Tim, I have noticed a couple of things right off the bat. Let us just get these two issues out of the way first, okay?" Tim nods. "First of all, you started off talking about this Vickie woman instead of your daughter's kidnapping. Isn't that a little odd that this would be more prominent in your mind? Secondly, this story about returning a wallet and then getting beat up by gang kids does not have a ring of truth to it. Matter of fact, it sounds like a similar story I read in a novel once. So let me recommend we start over with the truth this time, okay? I can't help you if you are not honest with me."

Tim gazes at the astute observations Tammy has made and says, "Hmmm, um, well, okay. The problem is Vickie and always has. It even overshadows the kidnapping because she was the one that rescued my daughter and killed the kidnapper, but then tried to blame me for the crime. Now my wife is not sure I am innocent or not. I originally was involved because I like Vickie and wanted to have an affair with her. I followed her to her house and she thought I was an attacker and defended herself to the point of beating me up. I tried to convince her I was not a bad guy and just wanted to leave it alone when she decided to make me pay for this incident." Tim stares, hoping there is enough truth in his lies to convince the therapist.

Tammy looks at him a bit and says, "That seems more logical and truthful. Did you go to the police and tell them what Vickie did?" Tim says he did not. "Well, you know, Tim, I am bound by law to tell law enforcement what I know involving a crime, especially murder. But I do believe you when you say you think this woman did this." Tim agrees the police should know and Tammy says, "Well, this is a good start for us. I'll let you go now and come to see me next week at this time, okay?" Tim agrees and leaves.

The next week, Tim goes to his next therapy session with Tammy. Tammy sits down and says, "Tim, I talked to the police. They said that they felt your story was out of desperation and they did not believe it. But that does not mean you are not telling the truth. How about we explore this Vickie person together and figure out why it has you so twisted up emotionally? I think once we get this handled, your other issues with marriage and so forth will fall in line."

"Well, like I said last time, she thought I was an attacker and hurt me badly. She is quite physical and has a black belt in something or another. Anyway, the next thing I know, she is friends with my wife, coming over for dinner, and now my daughter's scout leader. My daughter will be with her in a few weeks for summer camp and my wife is going to stay at her mom's for that week. Vickie tells me she and I have a lot to work out before she leaves me alone. To be honest, I was scared of her and then angry, but now I am getting depressed about it."

"I see. Have you ever thought about filing a restraining order against Vickie?"

"I can't, I mean, I am afraid of her."

"You can't because this woman has something over you as to why you can't get rid of her. Seems like an awful lot of revenge feelings on her part for you just showing up at her house. Sounds to me like maybe you did go over to her house for ill intentions and she got the better of you. Now she wants you to suffer for what you tried."

Tim has eyes the size of saucers looking back as he stutters, "I-I just wanted to meet her. She is beautiful and I got horny, is all. Maybe I was a little forward in meeting her, but that was it."

Tammy says, "Hmmm. Do you think Vickie would talk to me? Maybe I can clear up some things with her, get her to leave you alone."

Tim quietly says, "Yeah, maybe."

Tammy hands a pad of paper to Tim and asks him to write down Vickie's information, which he does. Tammy says, "Let's continue next week after I have a chance to talk with Vickie. I think next week we will get some good results and get you back to feeling happy."

Tim cautiously says, "Sure, thanks, Doctor."

All week Tim goes through the routine of work and home life with Lana having little to say or do with him. He has been particularly preoccupied with the next meeting with his therapist. Finally the day has come and at her office he is greeted.

"Come in, Mr. Jenkins."

Tim is feeling uneasy as he thinks to himself, *No Tim this time.*

Tammy says, "I talked to Miss Newsome and got some insight to this event. She claimed you stalked her from a bookstore to her house and somehow gained entry into her house without her knowing about it. She says after she comes out of the shower you threatened her life and wanted to rape her. She defended herself and out of fear she managed to hit you a few times but you managed to get her down. You told her that you would be back and that you were obsessed with her. If she did not comply with your wishes to be around you and your family in every way possible, including troop leading your daughter, you would harm her. Mr. Jenkins, I have been a psychiatrist for twenty years and I have never seen a more fearful woman in my life. I asked Miss Newsome about getting her help and she said it was okay, you had been leaving her alone lately. She had notified law enforcement about you already and had family watching out for her. She actually asked that I help you as much as I can."

Tim is sitting like a crumbling statue and says, "My God."

"Mr. Jenkins, I really don't want to help you any further so I would ask that you leave my office now and not return."

Tim says, "Okay, but she is lying and I have told you the truth."

Tammy replies, "Mr. Jenkins, you admitted you stalked her and was after her and had lied to me prior to that so your story is just not credible."

Tim walks out like he is walking a walk of shame and confusion. He returns home to find his wife as cold as ever to him.

A Break in the Ice

He goes to the park to sit and think about it all. A voice from behind him says, "Hey, Timmy boy, how was therapy?" He looks back and Vickie stands over him and then walks around and sits next to him.

Tim says, "Why can't you leave me alone? I am losing everything I feel. What do you want from me?"

Vickie looks around. "You know what I want? I want my childhood back. I want to not have been attacked by you and my relative that raped me as a teenager. I want to know that the child I had been grew up happy and safe after it was taken away from me and adopted." Vickie starts crying as Tim looks over at her. Vickie continues, "I want to have a normal life and not have to defend myself against people like you. I wished I did not have to be so physically fit to be able to overcome a man's strength. I want to have a relationship with a man without wondering if he is trustworthy. I don't want to be so pretty so men like you would not stalk me." Vickie looks at Tim with eyes wet and nose sniffling. She gets up and as she leaves, she turns to say, "I hate that you made me this way."

Vickie leaves abruptly as Tim whispers to himself, "I'm sorry, Vickie." Tim sits there staring at the birds and hearing them sing. He has a lot to process as the balance of the day draws to a close.

Weeks pass and Tim watches his daughter go off to summer camp as his work is done for several months too. Lana packs up and leaves for her mom's, not giving any good-bye or anything to her husband. Tim has spent his time researching some things and goes on his own adventure. Lana arrives at her mom's and embraces her tightly. She settles in for the week and begins to talk to her mom.

Lana says, "Mom, tell me about the time Tim and I dated? Why did Dad hate him so much then?"

Her mom says, "Sweetie, your dad did not trust him. He always seemed to be watching you more than just a young guy in love. He even talked to his parents and there were things that your dad just did not like about him. He even tried to bribe him to go away but he would not leave. Especially when he found out that he had been molested as a child. He just felt that he had too many issues."

Lana replies, "Maybe he was right all along. Mom, I am not sure I love him anymore. Maybe I fell out of love long ago, I don't know. I tried to stay with him and keep up appearances. For the most part I was content. But he seemed to be distant the last couple of years and spent a lot of time away after his work. Then this whole thing with Vickie happened and then the kidnapping. I just don't know. I think he is having an affair or had one with Vickie because they seem so tied together somehow and he is not being truthful with me about why that is. Also, everyone we know thinks he murdered that kidnapper."

Mom replies, "What do you think?"

Lana looks up. "I don't know, Mom. I really don't. I want to believe he did not kill that guy, but if he didn't I almost blame him for saying he did not. I have a hard time believing Vickie and he had an affair, but obviously they both are involved emotionally for some reason. I am so confused and I just don't think I can go on with him anymore."

Her mom replies, "Well, just relax here and it will sort out when you have some time to meditate on it."

Lana smiles and goes to her old room to look at her old stuff kept the way it was when she was young.

The week has almost passed and Lana is back at home to greet Tanya with Tim. Tanya comes back excited and happy to see them. They go back in the house to play the part of family members once again. Tim sits down with Tanya and asks her how the camp week went. Tanya said she learned how to hunt from Vickie and defend herself against predators. Tanya says, "I will never be kidnapped again. I can depend on myself to know what to do next time."

Tim says, "Uh, that is good. Go and play now."

He goes to the bedroom and sits on the bed next to his wife. Tim asks, "So how are you doing, honey?"

Lana looks at him and then looks away. "Have a lot to think about. I really don't want to discuss it."

Tim, disappointed, gets up and says, "Okay, but I love you and always will."

Lana does not acknowledge him and keeps looking at her magazine. The charade of family life continues day after day.

Tim sits down at a lonely dinner table eating a microwave dinner as his daughter is at a friend's for the day. Lana comes in from the backyard after a time pacing. She sits down at the dinner table and stares fiddling with the placemats. Tim continues to eat wondering what will be said. Tim makes small talk. "It was nice today."

Lana looks up. "Tim, I feel like I have been living on autopilot for almost a decade. I am not sure of myself anymore. It is not all your fault, but there is a lot I put up with."

Tim nods yes and looks around. "Whatever you need, I will do for you."

Lana looks at him and goes to the kitchen. The evening fades with not much of any interaction.

Two Can Play at this Game

The next day, Tim gets a call he has been waiting for and tells his wife he needs to go out of town for a few days.

She replies, "Whatever, Tim, go have fun."

Tim is saddened by her lack of interest, but he knows he must go on his mission. A few days pass and Tim arrives at Vickie's house on a Saturday and asks if she will escort him to do something he wants. Vickie is intrigued by this and agrees. They go to the bookstore that they both have frequented and Tim earnestly looks around while Vickie follows him, asking, "What are we looking for, Tim?"

Finally he spots what he has been seeking and says, "Her. What do you think? She looks pretty, does she not?"

Vickie looks at the young woman and says, "Yes, she is pretty. Are you going to stalk her too?"

Tim laughs and says, "Yes, c'mon."

Vickie is starting to get upset that he brought her to participate in finding a victim. He follows the young woman as Vickie follows him waiting to pounce on him at the first moment of indiscretion. Finally the girl sits at a café table outside and Tim sits down next to her. Vickie sits down too and apologizes for her friend's rudeness. The girl is staring at Vickie without saying a word. Vickie is confused and looks at Tim.

Tim says, "Vickie, this is Veronica…your daughter. I found her and brought her here."

Vickie looks back at Veronica and says, "That was my grandmother's name."

At that moment Veronica pulls out a picture of Vickie as a teenager, the only possession of her mom she had and says, "Mommy!"

They both jump up crying and hugging at the most emotional reunion possible. Tim stands up and slowly leaves with a smile. Vickie notices him leaving and runs over to him. "Tim, thank you."

He smiles and leaves, seeing Vickie and Veronica walk away catching up on years lost between a mother and daughter. As they walk, Vickie says, "Veronica, I never stopped thinking about you all these years. It was so hard—"

She is stopped by Veronica as she says, "Mom, Mr. Jenkins told me about you being raped as a young teenager and having to give me up. When he came to tell me about you, I was angry, but my curiosity about you could not keep me from listening. I know you had no choice and my parents, my adopted parents, were very loving and good to me. I only had one thing if I ever met you to ask. Why did you not come and find me?"

Vickie stared at the ground, pondering how to tell her and finally she says, "You know, I was lost and confused for a number of years and to be honest I was lost in myself. When I did find my identity I thought about you, actually all the time. I did ask people that my mom sent you to but records were locked and never allowed to be seen without court orders. No court would allow me to see them. I tried again a few years later after college when my career was starting. But it was to no avail, even with lawyers. Eventually I got involved with my life and career, somewhere I gave up hope. It appears between the rape and losing you is the reason I delved into my job and martial arts so heavily. Trying to fill a void that can never be filled. I'm sorry, so sorry. I never stopped thinking about you and hoping."

Veronica tearfully replies, "Mom, I forgave you long ago. I just lived disappointed I guess that I never got to know you. But I always felt you were out there somewhere. When I was thirteen, my adopted mom gave me your picture and told me what she knew about you. You don't have anything to make up to me, what is important is we have the rest of our lives to be with each other."

Vickie asks, "How did you get so smart as young as you are?"

Veronica smiles. "I had good genes. On my mom's side, that is!"

"What do you do? You are twenty-two, in college?"

"I wanted to go but my parents never had the money and the thought of a huge debt to pay off for many years just scared me."

"I am a marketing executive at an advertising company. It is a good job and I highly recommend it. The only drawback is when things are tight, marketing and sales people are usually the first to get axed. But luckily the company I am with is very stable. What do you want to do in life, Veronica?"

"I like astronomy but I was never really good in math. Not sure what I want to do in life really. I work at a department store mainly looking at guys wondering which one will sweep me off my feet. It is silly, I know."

"No, it is not silly, it is normal, I think. For me it was never in the cards obviously, tragically. You really need to think about an education because even if you find Mr. Right, something can happen and you may have to earn for yourself or family. Believe it, it is much easier to get an education when you are young and have fewer ties then older."

"I know what you are saying but it just takes too much to go."

"You know, Veronica, if you go to college I will pay for it."

With a shocked look, Veronica replies, "I can't take that from you. That is too much to ask anyone, and money you worked for."

"What am I going to spend it on? New car, new house, vacations? There gets a point in your life when things are not that important. Money does not bring happiness, only convenience. The only thing that really matters is people. You are my daughter and I lost over twenty years of your life, I can't let you lose more years of doing what you don't like doing."

Veronica lights up and gives Vickie a deep hug, telling her how much she loves her. They walk off with Veronica explaining about stars, galaxies, and everything astronomical. Vickie understands vaguely what she is talking about but is happy listening to her daughter talk about her passion.

Facade Falls

Tim comes home and Lana is sitting in the living room smoking a cigarette. He is puzzled and asks her, "Honey, when did you start smoking?"

"I have smoked while you were at work and our daughter was at school for a long time. It helps me deal with the day and the day that is coming."

"You seemed so happy, it was all but an act?"

"No, Tim, we had good times but I guess I was bored at times. You always seem to go off and do your thing while I sat at home taking care of Tanya."

"You were free to go out and I could watch her, we have a babysitter too."

"No, I did not want to leave her alone all the time. I want to be here for her. I still love you, I am just not happy."

"Look, I know we have been through hell lately but let's—"

Lana cuts him off. "I had an affair."

Tim, shaking his head fast, says, "What?"

"Three years ago, you were out on your summer trip with your teacher buddies. I was in the store and a young guy working there kept trying to pick me up. I laughed it off and told him I was happily married. I wasn't happily married and that resulted in loneliness. Maybe feeling a little older than I really was, I went back and began to talk to him. One thing leads to another and I dropped our daughter off with the babysitter and met the young man. Before I knew it we were in bed together. I cried on the way home and you know why? I felt guilty but also felt good and that made me feel bad. I never went back to that store again. But I did think about that evening, more than one occasion. I guess maybe that is what kept me married to you all this time since after I was feeling guilty. Well, are you going to say something or just stare at me like normal?"

"Look, I know I have not been an ideal husband and I really can't judge you because I am flawed like anyone, maybe more. Tell me what to do and let me fix it."

"Tim, you always want to fix things. I have made up my mind, I want a divorce. I don't want you to fight with me over custody. You would get visitations but I want us out."

Tim spins around slowly, despondent. "Please, don't leave me. I can't live without my family."

"It is too late, Tim. I have made up my mind. I want to start over while I still can." Lana gets up and leaves for the bedroom as Tim drops in his chair and begins to cry over all of it.

Tim is powerless as he watches Lana pack things as Tanya is already staying at her grandmother's house. Movers come to carry boxes as Lana is finishing up from days of packing. The only interaction between her and Tim is to ask about items, whether he wanted them or not. Tim is only left with pictures in frames of him and Lana and furniture she will not need. She carries the final box to her car and loads it in the backseat. Movers start their truck and wait to follow her. Lana stares at the box holding the back door open as Tim walks up behind her. She turns and gives him a hug and kisses him on the cheek, walking to the driver side of the car. She stops and stares at Tim as he closes the back door for her. She manages to make a half smile and gets in the car. Tim backs away as they all leave. His eyes are fixed on the caravan as they turn leaving his sight. Neighbors stare from behind pulled window curtains and begin to go about their business. Tim looks up at the sun and walks back into his house. He stares at the rooms and remembers the voices and times spent with his wife and kid. Like a ghost, he wanders to and fro, haunting each area with his memories. Finally, as time passes, it sets in that he is alone.

The Hole You Leave Behind

Time has passed and the school year has started. Tim is working, still living in his house as Lana and Tanya have moved on living in Lana's mom's house, and Tim did not contest anything in the divorce. He sits in the park he frequented and stares at the autumn leaves falling off the trees. It is like his life, everything dying off and falling. He feels that he has brought this all on himself holding his face in his hands, when he hears a familiar voice.

"Hello, stranger."

Tim looks around to see Vickie, and says, "I don't care anymore, do what you want."

Vickie sits down next to him. "Tim, it is over between us. What you did for me and my daughter I could never repay you."

"That is wonderful, you gain your daughter and I lose mine." Vickie looks confused. "Lana divorced me and took Tanya. I am all alone now. Seems she was unhappy for a long time and I did not know it."

"I know she was, Tim. She told me. At the time I was so in the mode of seeking revenge against you, I did not care. Now I have come to realize that revenge makes both parties pay, not just the person targeted."

"I guess that is why God says revenge is his because he is the only one living above karma."

"I suppose so."

They are quiet for a while feeling the cool breeze blow on them. Tim says, "Hey, how are things with your daughter?"

Vickie smiles. "She is good, we are good. She is going to college to study Astronomy and Astrophysics. Can you believe that? It is like a dream come true that was unimaginable." Vickie looks at Tim staring at the ground quietly. "Look, Tim, I am so sorry for everything. You know you are welcome to hang out with me."

Tim smiles and laughs. "You know, it was not all that long ago you were chasing me out of your house. How can you trust me now?"

Vickie looks at Tim intently. "You've changed from not being a monster, you changed back to what you were, a human being. I trust you, as long as you don't pull any funny stuff, ha-ha!"

Tim smiles. "I think I just want to be in solitude now but I am glad you are happy and wish the best for your daughter."

"All right, Tim, I respect that. You know where to find me if you need anything."

"Thank you, Vickie. Have a good life, okay?"

Vickie leaves, nodding her head yes and looks back once in a while leaving. Tim remains staring at the trees and feeling the disintegration of his life. Tim becomes withdrawn more and more as his work suffers. Students have to ask him numerous times as he seems to be in another world. The school sends him home, substituting him frequently with other teachers but he never comes back better. Finally he is called into the office and told he is being dismissed effective immediately. Tim goes home after and brings a bottle of cheap liquor and drinks his way into unconsciousness. He seems to drown in bottles as weeks go by and bills not being paid, first utilities disconnected and then foreclosure. He sleeps in the park as his car was repossessed, being roused once in a while to move on by authorities. He wanders streets and passes by the old bookstore he frequented. He no longer sees attractive women but patrons buying books he can no longer afford to buy. His credit goes bad, bank account dries up, and with little cash on him, he makes his way to a homeless shelter. They feed him and give him a place to rest for the night but he must leave during the day. He spends his time under bridges and his mind is a blank with no ambition, no memories, just the instinct to lie down. He feels the inevitability of death but day after day seems to keep living despite his giving up. He wakes to college boys peeing on him and laughing as he mumbles threats. Another evening comes and it is time to go eat whatever and shelter for the night. He arrives and stares at the shelter as tears roll down. He walks away and finds a bridge over a lake. Staggering and disoriented, he is going to end it all. He walks to the edge of the bridge and a hand reaches and touches his shoulder. He turns to what thinks is a hallucination of a Valkyrie.

"Tim, I have been looking all over for you. What do you think you are doing?"

It is Vickie. Tim says, "Leave me alone for once, will you? I just want to end it. The pain is too much. No one loves me and I am nothing but a damn rapist."

"Not anymore, you are not. Come with me and I will prove it."

She walks him to the car and starts to drive him to her house. As they drive, Tim says, "Why do you care? Why does anyone care?"

"Look, Tim, this is not a Lazarus game I am playing with you. People care because we can all end up in the shape you are in. You just need some good food and good rest. But first you are getting hosed off, whew!"

Vickie rolls down the window as Tim chuckles a little. Vickie smiles and says, "See, I knew you were still in there."

Tim whimpers, "Yeah," as he utters a bitter weak cry. Tim asks, "What is a Lazarus game?"

"It is a game executives play with the down and out, it is terrible real life game. Let's not talk about it, okay?"

Tim stares out the window as they travel quietly. They arrive at her house and she cleans him up and gives him soup to eat. Later, he sleeps from what seems to be noon the next day. Getting up and wandering to the living room where Vickie and Veronica are, he sits down.

Veronica says, "Hi, Mr. Jenkins."

Tim says, "Oh, hey, it is good to see you. I thought you were in school."

Vickie says, "Tim, it is the holidays, school is out."

"Oh, okay. What holiday?"

Vickie and Veronica look at each other and Veronica says, "Thanksgiving. Tomorrow is Thanksgiving."

"Oh, already?"

Vickie says, "Tim, you can stay with me till you get back on your feet. And you will get back on your feet!"

Veronica says, "Mom?"

Vickie looks at her daughter. "Okay, just take it easy, Tim."

The next day they all sit down to a nice Thanksgiving meal. Veronica looks around and says, "You know, it is almost like a picture perfect family."

Tim says, "Yeah, a lost child, a victim, and—"

Vickie stops him. "Tim, relax and let us just enjoy this day."

"You're right, I'm sorry. The food is beautiful."

The next day Vickie comes home to Veronica laughing with Tim and talking astronomy. Days pass and Tim is getting better and Veronica has gone back to school.

Rock Bottom Phoenix

As music plays in the background softly, Tim and Vickie are relaxed sitting on the floor talking about daily things. The atmosphere grows serious and quiet when Vickie asks, "Tim, Lana had told me some things about your childhood and what happened to you. It might do you some good to talk about it, not like I don't know you all too well now anyway."

Tim stares and casually looks at his drink. "You know, I had a very typical upbringing. My parents were simple people and we lived in a quiet community. The community was like a vast subdivision but with few houses, so it was a kid's paradise, lots of empty woods to run around in and little vehicle traffic. I wandered all over the hillsides, up and down streets and golf courses. I did not have many friends so I spent a lot of time by myself. I had a bicycle but many times I just walked around. One day, when I was in fifth grade, I passed by a house and the garage was open with a man working in it. He was in his fifties, it seemed. At that age he was old but in very good shape. His garage was full of tools and car parts. I had seen him before and knew of him. I knew his wife worked at the school as a secretary. Everybody liked her. Anyway, he said hello to me and I said hi back. He asked where I lived and I told him. He told me he knew who my parents were. Then he asked me if I would like to see something interesting he is working on. He was very cordial and soft spoken so I did not feel threatened at all. He showed me some small engine parts he was putting together and went into detail about it. It was interesting and I suppose I ate the attention up. Once in a while he would ask me if I had a girlfriend and that he bet I was looking forward to having fun with girls. I really didn't grasp anything was wrong, just thought he was playing around. He asked if I would like to see what they look like a little older without clothes and showed me an adult magazine. Of course I said sure. He said he had to close the garage door so no one can see and asked me if I can keep it a secret. I acknowledged the deal and he showed me these gorgeous naked ladies and his trick to get me excited was working.

"He then asked me if I had ever masturbated. I knew what he was talking about but he said he would teach me. He put the magazine down with the centerfold open on the table and pulled down his pants. I was feeling uncomfortable and he could tell. He was so slick about asking me if I was okay and that this is between us two boys. He began stroking himself and explaining how it works. He then told me to try it and stared at me quietly till I got the nerve to take my pants off. He then took all his clothes off and put them on the table and told me to do the same so we don't get them dirty. He began stroking himself and told me to follow along, which I did."

Vickie gasps and says, "Oh my God, that is terrible."

Tim looks around and starts to tear up.

Vickie says, "Tim, it is okay, this is where you heal."

Tim looks at Vickie and down to the ground and shakes his head yes. He continues, "He acted like I was doing it wrong and told me he would show me and grabbed my wrist to help me stroke while his other hand was on my butt. He then moved my hand away to show me and grabbed my penis and gently rubbed it and my back simultaneously. He told me not to be scared, that guys do this all the time. It is how they learn to deal with girls. I was so in shock by what was happening I guess I was in denial and believing all this crap he was telling me. He then got on his knees and leaned over to perform oral sex. My heart was racing like a horse until I finished. I felt cross-eyed and dizzy. He told me that it was my turn and to get on my knees. He then had me perform oral sex on him until he was done. Then he cleaned both of us up as I was feeling sick to my stomach. After getting dressed, I told him I wanted to go home now. His demeanor changed from the soft spoken gentleman to threatening. He said that if I told anyone what happened he would kill my parents and then me. There would be no place for me to hide from him. I was so scared of him at this point as he showed me a machete. He made me repeat that I understood three times and I was crying. He then said okay and opened the garage. I walked out slowly looking back as he stared at me and as I got to the end of his driveway he simply started working on that engine part again."

Tim started crying as tears rolled down Vickie's face as well. "It is okay, Tim."

"I went home and went straight to bed and did not talk to anyone for weeks. After months I began playing with myself regularly but strangely I did not think about him or what happened to me, I just thought about girls. It was like the event never happened and eventually I seemed to get a back to normal. Years later, there was a kid in around my age, about fifteen years old that I knew. He lived in the town nearby but for the summer was staying over at that man's house. We played around and he wanted to go to the swimming pool and asked me to stop by this man's house he was staying at. I was older and felt I was strong enough to deal with it and I did go. But as I walked up to this man's house, it was like gravity was getting stronger and harder to walk. I finally managed to come to the door and rang the bell but stood back a few feet. My friend answered the door and said he would be out in a few minutes. I walked to the end of the driveway and waited but intently looking at the man's garage, which looked just as junky as it did years prior. All of a sudden the man stepped out in to the garage and grabbed an oil rag and started cleaning some part. He just stared at me with cold evil eyes and never said a word. I stared back and the fear washed over me like a waterfall. The emotions and whole experience just came back to me like it just happened. He never spoke, just stared. Through the front door my friend ran out to me and yelled back to the man, 'Bye and I will be back soon.' We walked off and my friend asked me if I knew the man. I told him that I never met him. He was talking about how his parents had to work out of town and this man and his wife took him in as well as other people did with his siblings for the summer to help his parents. I asked my friend if this man ever… but I was at a loss for words. I dropped the subject and we began just talking normal things for teenagers. I never told my parents what happened nor anyone else for that matter."

Vickie asks, "What ever happened to that bastard of a man?"

Tim smiled for a moment. "You don't mince words, do you? Apparently that man made a move on my friend that summer but my friend had more courage than I and resisted him and told his parents. I remember hearing that the man's wife was told at school her husband had been arrested and she passed out. It was the last we ever saw of her or him. I had heard that they moved to where no one knew them. Later I learned that my friend's brother had stayed years prior around the time I had my event with this man and his brother grew up gay. This was a huge issue for my friend's family as they were very religious. But they accepted their son as did my friend. The man died years later. I felt a sense of relief that he was gone. Even though I was an adult when he died, it was like the threat was gone."

Tim smiled and suddenly looked down at the floor crying. "He took my childhood from me! I did not know how to have relationships with girls after that. I was so awkward and always suspicious of people. I just wanted to be normal."

Vickie grabs Tim and hugs him as he just seemed to bellow like a small child. Eventually Tim calmed down and asks, "You know, Vickie, the worse thing? I almost wanted it to happen again, not with that man but with someone nonthreatening. I hated myself for that. I just wanted to kill myself about it."

"You felt ashamed, like you did something wrong, you did something to deserve it. But what you were craving was not so much the sex act but the adrenaline and feeling that came from it again. It is addictive, like a drug. Some people do go back to it and want to feel that high again. I think maybe that is why you tried to attack me. All these years it was pinned up inside you waiting to be dealt with. You did not have a chance with Lana to fulfill your deep emotional needs because she actually liked you and married you. You gave up on trying to live that fantasy out, at least for a while till you met me. I understand this, Tim, very well. You see I went through a lot of therapy from my attack years ago as a teenager."

Tim's eyes lifted up and he says, "You know, I feel like a huge weight has been lifted off me."

"It is a confessional relief is what you are experiencing. There is something therapeutic about telling your issues to another person. It brings it out and removes the guilt and shame of it. If people had someone to talk to and let out their problems or even their psychotic fantasies, it would help them not to try to live them out. Maybe we would have less office and school shootings if people were more involved and communicating with the loners."

"You're right, it would make a big difference. I wished I had done this long ago. So, Vickie, it is your turn, what happened to you?"

"I was afraid you were going to say that." Tim smiles as Vickie smirks. "Okay, my childhood was not really rosy like yours. My dad was an alcoholic and my mom just took his shit all the time. He was abusive to her and used to hit her, but she never told anyone and always told me to keep it to myself. I hated him so much, I just wanted to kill him. When things in life at our home were really bad, Mom would often send me to an older cousin's house to stay for a day or two. I would come home and Mom would have a new bruise or two on her. When I got to age twelve, I began to talk back to my dad and scream at him to leave Mom alone. He never hit me but always made the motion of doing it. It just seemed to make things worse the more I spoke up. One time he beat Mom so bad, it put her in the hospital and I never spoke to my dad voluntarily again, I just shut up. My cousin and his wife were married and had kids of their own. They were nice and it was like night and day compared to our household. My cousin would play chess with me and talk to me. We were very close, it was like the dad I wished I had. I stayed for several weeks one summer, I was sixteen and it was not a very sweet sixteen. No car, no gifts, I was just ignored. My cousin took me out and taught me how to drive a car and had a little fun spinning tires in it. We went to a park that was empty and talked for the longest while. The day was dying out and as we talked he kissed me. I was blushing and shocked because he was in his thirties and my cousin but I loved him like a dad. He tried to kiss me again, but I pushed him away and said no. He withdrew and apologized and told me that I was so beautiful he simply could not resist. I blushed and told him I understood.

We went back to his house and it seemed like everything was normal, like nothing happened. I felt safe that it would never happen again.

"Several days passed by and his wife and kids went to an event at her parents all day. My cousin and I played chess and he got me a drink of soda and as the game progressed I got very dizzy. He asked me if I was all right and the next thing I knew I was laying on my bed. I felt really groggy and he came in the room and handed me water. He said that I passed out and he carried me to bed after talking with a doctor. The doctor said I needed rest. I remember looking at the clock and a few hours had passed. He left the room and I drank the glass of water and started to get my senses back. I felt something was wrong and felt a stinging pain in my groin. As I went to the bathroom it was hurting more and I realized I had been raped. When I came back into the living room, he was all jolly and asked how I was doing. I just acted like things were okay and sat away from him watching TV with him in the corner of my eye. Later that night, I cried because I knew I had no one to tell, he was my only friend. If I told his wife he might beat her like my dad does my mom. I felt trapped and alone. As weeks passed I became reclusive and depressed. My mom knew something was wrong, especially since I never wanted to go back to our cousin's anymore. For the first time in a long time, she began to talk to me as a mom and I confided in her that I was raped by my cousin. I explained the whole event and what happened. She told me she was going to take me to the doctor the next day. We did go and I was given a pregnancy test. Later the doctor told us it was positive. Mom told me we had to tell Dad because I was going to show before too long. I was terrified at the prospect of that. But we all sat down and Mom explained everything. Dad asked me if I was acting like a little whore around my cousin. I cried and told him no we just played chess and he taught me to drive a car and nothing. He drugged me and raped me. Dad told me he did not believe me and that I was a little whore just like my mother. He got up, went to the bedroom, and got his gun. My mom screamed, asking what he was doing. He told her he was going to kill that bastard for screwing his whore daughter. Mom pleaded with him not to go, but there was no stopping him. As he drove off she called my cousin's wife and told her what was going on. She then told my cousin and by the time my dad got there and kicked open their door my cousin killed him with a shotgun."

Tim's eyes are like saucers as he says, "Damn! I am so sorry."

"I was devastated hearing my dad was killed but at the same time relieved that he would never hurt my mom again or have to deal with his shit again. My cousin was arrested and got probation. The police grilled me and my mom about the reasons my dad went over but we never told them why and my cousin and his wife never did either. The police simply ruled it an alcoholic rage. Times were hard for us as mom had to work to support us. We had no savings, no insurance, and Dad left us nothing to survive on. I was so scared to be a mommy myself as a teenager and my mom had no way to support another child. She made me put my child up for adoption. As soon as the baby was born, I got to see her for a few minutes and she was taken away. I never knew who got her and what happened. I felt empty and thought about my baby for years. When you brought her back in my life, I went and visited the parents who raised her and they were awesome. It is like I have another family now through them. They are so wonderful. My mom passed on a year later of a heart attack and she really was not that old. I guess the stress of her life wore on her. I miss her so. My cousin died of prostate cancer many years later. I never saw him again. I guess I shed myself of my whole past and started anew. I managed to put myself through college and did very well in my career. Basically I spent all my time on my career and making myself strong and never defenseless again."

Tim says, "I can attest to that."

Vickie laughs as he smiles.

"You know, Vickie, I never thanked you for saving my life. I did a lot of thinking and you saved me twice, one from the bridge and the other from my issues just now. I think I knew deep down that my marriage was a sham. I married the object of my obsession not affection, and she eventually knew it too. I did not know what love is or even how to emulate it correctly. It took me hitting rock bottom to see things clearly. I think I finally for once in my life know who I am and what I want. I feel actually good."

Vickie raises her glass and says, "Here is to us, Tim, two imperfect creatures that came out of the fire of life only to temper ourselves stronger."

Tim raises his. "And to our future, now that we honestly know ourselves and what made us, so we can now use those things that harmed us to do something positive."

Vickie says, "Hear, hear," as they drink. The night dies out quietly as they retire for the evening.

Rebuilding in Time

Vickie comes in from work and finds food laid out on the table that Tim has been working on for a while obviously. Vickie says, "This is nice, Tim."

Tim pulls the chair out for her and says, "I got a job. A teacher had health issues and they needed someone to fill in for the rest of the year."

"That is great!"

As they eat, Tim says, "I owe you a lot, Vickie. I feel like I have a purpose in life and need to do something to give back."

"That is good, Tim. You can do anything you want in life. The only thing that gets in the way of your goals is you."

"You know, Vickie, there is no telling what I would have been if my childhood would have been happier."

"That is crap, Tim. You are telling me that an emotion about something that happened to you long ago is sabotaging your life now? You probably don't even remember your childhood as it really happened correctly, just how you feel about it. Just imagine that you had a great childhood and that feeling will go away."

"You know, you are right."

They eat as if they were two old friends. As time progresses, Tim finds an apartment to live in and works with a new sense of purpose. Tim has become a regular fixture hanging out with Vickie and becoming good friends. All seems well as months pass and he visits with his daughter. Spending time in his favorite park, helping with the soup kitchen that used to support him. Vickie comes to his home one evening.

Tim says, "About time you came over here. How you like my new pad?"

"It is nice, Tim. Look, Tim, sit down, we need to talk."

Tim looks puzzled as he sits down. "Tim, Lana's mom called me because she knew we were friends. Lana had my phone number and so she called me. Tim, Lana is in the hospital. She is sick with breast and lung cancer. Apparently it was undiagnosed and spread from her lungs from smoking. It has been going on for a while and Lana did not want you to know till now. It is not good and she does not have much time. Her mom wanted you to know because she has been asking about you. She is at her mom's house, like a hospice."

As he drives, he is thinking about all the times he and Lana had and about their daughter Tanya. He spends the evening and the hours driving till he arrives at Lana's mom's house. He arrives at night and as he gets out of his car, it takes him back to the time he first followed Lana here. The feelings overwhelm him as he walks up the walkway as if cinderblocks were on his shoes. Before he can reach the door, Tanya runs out of the front door.

"Daddy!" She hugs him tightly crying. They walk to the house and up the stairs to Lana's room where Lana lays in her bed with her mom comforting her. Lana's mom hugs Tim and tells him she will get his favorite drink as she leaves the room with Tanya. Tim stands by the bed and Lana, weakened and pale, looks at him quietly and with all her might to tell him to sit down next to her. He sits on the bed with tears rolling down his face not sure what to say.

He says, "I got a new job at another school, a charter school. Little easier than public."

Lana smiles. "I'm glad. I'm proud of you. I never stopped loving you."

"Me neither, I think about you often."

Lana wearily pats his arm. "Tim, this is important. Take Tanya and raise her well. She needs you now more than ever. Take care of her."

"Of course, honey, we will make our lives together."

Lana smiles as tears rolls out of her eyes; "Good, good. Tim, Tim…I know you did not kill that guy. You are a good man…Tim."

Tim smiles, then crying and looking at her night stand, he sees the book he gave her on their first date. He laughs and says, "Honey remember when I gave you this book?"

He turns and Lana is laying there with her eyes closed. "Lana? Honey? Sweetheart!" As no sign of life is in her anymore, he lays his head on her shoulder and cries. The sound of crying brings Tanya and her grandmother in the room and they all sit on the bed.

A year has passed since Lana's death and Tim and Tanya visit her grave. Tim has moved and got a job at a private school in his mother-in-law's town so Tanya can be close to her grandma. It has been a tough year of adjustments. Tanya says, "I wish Vickie was here."

Tim says, "I know, sweetie, but she lives in our old town and she has her own life with her daughter."

Tanya says, "I'm not supposed to tell you, but Vickie was the one that rescued me from my kidnapper."

"How do you know that?"

"When I was tied to the bed, I heard the fighting between her and the kidnapper. She told him that he was going to learn who the spider and who the fly really is. I recognized her voice. After the fight she came in the room and told me it was her and not to tell anyone she was there. The police would come soon to rescue her but it is important that no one including you know she was there."

Tim looked around and smiled "Thank you for trusting me with that. You know, Vickie helped me out too in many ways."

"How is that, Daddy?"

"Let's just say there are things that were done that seemed mean, but sometimes there are no bad experiences, only taken bad."

"I don't understand. Are not bad experiences bad?"

"Sweetie, it turns out that we learn more from negative experiences as positive ones are taken for granted. Intelligence helps us to realize things before we make mistakes, but we can't foresee all. No one is that smart, but even with smartness, emotion can overcome any intelligence. Understand?"

"I guess so. I just know I don't like bad things."

"I know, honey."

"Mom used to call me that."

"Well, you are sweet as honey."

"Thank you, Daddy."

Tanya and Tim headed for home.

They Grow Up So Fast

Tanya is grown to the point of learning to drive. Vickie has insisted that she teach her how to drive, as Tim gratefully agrees and takes his place in the backseat. Vickie gives instructions as Tim interjects once in a while.

Tanya says, "Dad, I love you but you're a backseat driver."

Tim says, "You're right honey, just listen to Vickie. Oh, and keep your head on a swivel."

"Dad! I am watching where I am going."

"I have faith in you, just worried about the other drivers."

"Dad!"

"Okay, okay"

Tim sits back as Vickie smiles at him and continues with her instruction.

"Miss Vickie, when did you learn to drive?"

Vickie pauses for a while giving her some instructions then responds, "I learned at your age from a relative."

"Was he patient like you or antsy like dad back there."

Tim says, "Hey, watch out there."

Vickie replies, "He was very patient, very patient."

Tim looks at Vickie's eyes in the rear view mirror as she said it softly. He can see pain in her eyes as she looks up and sees him and then looks away.

Tanya has earned her driver's permit and she and Tim go on a day trip to Vickie's to celebrate. Tanya says, "Look, Miss Vickie, I have my permit. Let me drive you around."

Tim says, "Go ahead, you two, I will hold down the fort."

Tanya and Vickie leave as Tim watches them drive off.

In the car, Tanya says, "I love driving. Dad told me if I got my license he would let me start dating. All my friends have been on dates but Dad is so protective."

Vickie says, "For good reason. There are a lot of bad people out there. When you are dating, just be sure to buy your own drinks, don't take any from your date."

"Why is that?"

"It is just best to get your own. Don't want the boy to think you are just using him, do you? Buy your own."

"It is okay if a boy buys me food unless you are afraid they are going to expect something from me later, or drug me."

"Look, just be careful."

Silence goes for a while when Tanya says, "Miss Vickie, thank you for saving me long ago. And I am sorry that I told Dad about it."

"I knew you would eventually. It is not good to hold that kind of a thing a secret anyway."

"I think about that day almost every day."

"I know. I have a few memories like that myself. It is important that you learn to catalogue it correctly in your mind and not let it run untamed doing who knows what to your emotions."

"I get it. Here we are."

Vickie gets out and invites them in for a movie. Tim replies, "Thank you, but no thanks. She insisted we come show you her new driving permit. But we need to get back."

Vickie says, "I understand. Good-bye, Tanya, and congratulations!"

"Thank you, Miss Vickie! Good-bye!"

Tanya and Tim drive off as Vickie waves.

Bad Boys

It is fall and school is fully underway while Tanya is now in eleventh grade. She attracts the attention of one of the school's bad boys, Dane Stevenson. Dane, one of the cool kids, dresses like he missed out on a couple of decades. Despite her friends telling her to stay away from him, she can't resist. He is confident and has a muscle car that his dad restored and gave to him. Tanya is taken in by the whole package. Dane's friends don't quite understand why he is involved with a brainy girl. But he tells her he loves her and she is naive to his obsession of her. However, the love affair turns sour as she begins to despise his tactics and breaks up with him. Instead of letting it go, he harasses her by driving by her home late at night and spinning his tires out. The prank phone calls and bullying at school begin to upset her, and she finally breaks down and asks her dad for help. He had promised her he would stay out of despite the issues he witnessed.

Tanya says, "Dad, please help me get rid of this guy. I broke up with him two weeks ago but he won't let it go."

"I have to be careful because as a teacher this could be trouble. I was hoping he would just go away but obviously he is fixated on you."

"I don't understand how a guy can just spend all their energy wanting someone like that."

"It is strange, I guess."

The next day, Tim approaches Dane. "Mr. Stevenson, can you do me a favor?"

Dane replies, "Sure, Mr. Jenkins."

"I need you leave my daughter alone okay. Find someone else."

"That I cannot do, Mr. Jenkins." Dane puts his arm around him and says, "Timothy, let me tell you something. I will leave Tanya alone when I am ready and there is nothing anyone can do about it."

Tim pushes his arm off him. "You listen to me, I can get you kicked off this campus if you are not careful."

"That does not harm me, just frees my time up."

Dane starts to walk off and points his finger like a gun at Tim. Tim goes into the principal's office to discuss Dane. After explaining the issue, the principal explains that Dane has been kicked out of several schools and is under a new second chance program. Unless he does a crime, the school really won't get involved with anything on him. Tim frustrated goes home and tells Tanya the news. She cries and goes to her room. Tim looks around and gives Vickie a call.

"Vickie, I have a problem and need your help." Tim explains the entire situation and then awaits for an answer back.

Vickie pauses for a bit and then says, "I will take care of it."

Tim thanks her as the conversation ends. Tanya is in class and looks over the next row of seats slightly behind her as Dane winks at her. She slowly turns around as the teacher says they have a guest speaker today. Then enters Vickie into the classroom. She is stunningly dressed as a cat call goes out from Dane. The teacher tells Dane to stop that and pay attention. The teacher introduces Vickie. "This is Miss Newsome here from an advertising business to discuss careers. You young men and women need to think about this seriously so please give Miss Newsome your full attention."

Dane says, "I sure will."

The teacher gives a bad look as Vickie steps up. "Hello, junior class, it is an honor to be here to speak to you."

Dane is scope locked on Vickie and she reciprocates back with stares of interest in Dane. Vickie says, "You mister?"

Dane responds, "Mister Stevenson."

"Very well, Mister Stevenson, what are your career plans?"

"Work on cars, what I do right now anyway."

"Bet you are good at that."

"Good at a lot of things."

"Really? That is impressive. I have some car issues myself and might have to see if you can diagnose what I need."

"Sure can, I can fix you right."

The teacher says cuts in and says, "That is enough, Dane, be respectful."

Vickie continues, "That is okay, a little fun is okay, don't you agree, Mister Stevenson?"

Dane just smiles as Vickie continues with a speech about careers once in a while looking at Dane with smiling eyes. Dane intently looks at Vickie, totally ignoring Tanya. Tanya is feeling like Vickie is her heroine again. Vickie ends her speech and leaves staring at Dane. The class ends soon after and Dane bypasses Tanya without any attention. Tanya sighs in relief and smiles at her friend next to her.

School ends and Dane approaches his car as Vickie walks up to him. Dane stops and says, "Hot Mamma, what a MILF."

Vickie stops and tugs on his jacket to straighten it out and says, "I'm no mother and I don't care what you like."

"You don't fool me, I know who you are. You are Vickie, Tanya used to brag about you. I've seen you with her."

"Really? What else did she tell you about me."

"You are a badass karate bitch. You try anything on me and I won't hesitate to hit a woman and then you get in trouble for fighting a minor."

"Got it all figure out, do you? Tell you what, if I start a fight with you I guarantee I will win. Because even if I lose that day, I keep coming back over and over even after I start winning. About you being a minor, who is going to believe a juvenile delinquent scumbag like you that you did not attack me. You have twenty classmates who saw you staring at me all during my speech and making innuendos at me."

"Who cares? They kick me out, I just go somewhere else."

"I am giving you fair warning to stay away from Tanya."

"Her dad sic you on me? Tell you what, you keep trying to scare me and I will keep fantasizing about you on your knees. As far as Tanya, we are not finished till I say we are finished, got it?"

Vickie is taken back a bit and says, "Okay." Vickie turns and leaves but turns around and says, "Enjoy the present I left for you at home."

Dane is surprised and says, "What the f—whatever."

Dane gets in his car and drives around, thinking about Vickie and her threats but his arrogance is such that it quickly wipes away the worry as he reaches home. He comes in and his dad says, "Boy, get in here, we have something to discuss."

"What, Dad?"

"What is this shit?" His dad holds up a bag of weed and says, "Didn't I give you that car on the promise you would not get involved with drugs again, boy?"

Dane gasps; "That is not mine, Dad, I swear. There is this bitch lady that likes my girlfriend and she told me there was a present waiting for me at home."

His dad replies, "Son, that is the biggest load of horse shit I have heard all week. I found this bag in your toolbox in the garage where you leave tools lying about as usual. You are telling me this woman came in our closed garage, put this bag of weed in there just to get at my seventeen-year-old dipshit son?"

"I swear to you, Dad, on Mom's grave, that is not mine and this Vickie woman is real."

"Well, let me just call your girlfriend and ask her." His dad dials Tanya's home as Tanya answers.

"Tanya, do you know a woman named Vickie?"

Tanya says, "No Mister Stevenson, I don't. Why do you ask?"

He replies, "Because my son claims there is an adult friend of yours named Vickie terrorizing him."

Tanya laughs. "That is silly, Mister Stevenson. I told Dane if he did not stop smoking dope he was going to hallucinate someday."

Dad looks at Dane angrily. "Really?"

"Yes, Mister Stevenson, and can you tell Dane that I am sorry he broke up with me but I am okay with it."

"I will, Tanya, good day!" He hangs the phone up as Tanya hangs hers up and she looks over at Tim and Vickie. They all smile and laugh very loudly. Meanwhile, Dane's dad says, "Listen to me, you little screwhead, your car is gone and you are going to rehab." Dane is visibly shook and upset, crying almost, as he pleads but his fate is sealed as he is out of the picture for a long time and kicked out of the school program he was in.

A New Start

A YEAR HAS passed and Tim is watching the graduation of Tanya from high school. It had been some years since her grandmother's death. But it is a proud moment, not a sad one as Tim hears Tanya give the valedictorian address. Tanya stands and speaks to the crowd.

"This is a day that we all move from learning the basics of education to life for some and more education for others. But no matter what path we choose, it is important to do what we love in life and then find a way to make a living at it. My inspirations have been a friend from my childhood, Vickie, my grandmother who unfortunately did not live to see me graduate, my mom, who also did not live to see this either but I know they are both watching me and proud. But mainly, my dad for always being there and never giving up on me during the most difficult times of my life. Dad, thank you for your guidance, love, care and for being a good father and a great teacher. Class! Let's bring it on!"

The other students roar with cheers and claps as Tim is teared up with joy and pride. After the graduation ceremonies, Tanya joins Tim and as they hug, Vickie shows up. Tanya runs over and hugs her, saying, "You made it!"

Vickie says, "I would not have missed this for the world."

Tim tells Vickie, "She has a scholarship and she wants to be—"

Tim looks at Tanya as Tanya says, "Business and Marketing."

Vickie says, "Wow, very nice. I can help you with that. You know my daughter graduated recently too, only took forever it seems because of the graduate work but she is an astronomer now."

Tim says, "That is awesome. What have you been doing lately?"

"Well, I am the CEO of our company now and we are doing very well."

"Well, lookee there, maybe, Tanya, she can give you a job later."

Vickie says, "You know, Tanya, you do well and I guarantee you a spot at my company."

Tanya says, "Thank you, Vickie, I won't let you down."

Vickie says, "Well, I am sorry I have to run but have to travel out of the country to visit some clients. I am on a tight schedule."

They both give Vickie hugs and watch her leave. Tim and Tanya feel blessed in their lives as they go to celebrate this day.

Tim has moved into Lana's parents' home after graduation and still keeps Lana's room as she was in it. He visits it once in a while and thinks about her. He looks at the book that he gave her on their first date. He thinks about the times and particularly focuses on the hints she was not happy. Feeling guilty and missing her greatly, he thinks to himself that life is a series of lessons and mistakes. But sometimes you can't lessen the pain but increase the mental tools to deal with it. He realizes that sometimes it is the impact of life's issues that first happen that sting the most and maybe there are ways to be prepared for what is ahead and bounce off issues right. Life seems to be 90 percent how you react to things will depend on what happens next. Life is hard enough without complicating it with drama and issues. Oftentimes, we simply create the issues we face just by the way we live.

He begins to feel like a new chapter has opened in his life and that now that his daughter is away in college, he has time to contemplate things. He goes into work at the local public school, engulfing himself not just in teaching but in many administrative tasks throughout the year. By the end of the school year, he is called into the principal's office.

Principal Dan Stouples has been there for many years and has liked Tim quite a bit.

Tim says, "Hey, Dan, what's up," as he enters the office.

"Tim! Come in and have a seat. You know, Tim, I have been in this game for a long time and I am wanting to retire this year."

"You deserve it, but this place won't be the same without you."

"How can it be the same? The problem I have is a successor. I was thinking of Daniels, maybe Samuels?"

"Daniels is good for sure and Samuels, well, if anyone can do this job she can. What about Sims?"

"Sims is an interesting choice, but I think we need some fresh blood in here. Actually I want to recommend you for my job to the board and the superintendent agrees with me."

"I'm honored, but I have not been here that long."

"Nonsense, you have been a teacher for years, you have the credentials and experience needed, and you bring some good ethics here. You are a good man and to be honest I did talk to the others and they actually recommended you for the job over themselves. Everybody likes you, Tim. Take a week and think about it."

Tim looks around and says, "You know what, I accept if it goes through."

They both get up and shake hands as Dan says, "Tim, you made my day. I can go fishing full time now. I will process everything and let you know, but I don't think there will be an issue."

Tim goes home and calls his daughter. "Honey they want me to be principal."

"Oh my God, Dad! That is awesome. You will do well there."

"I hope so, it is a lot of responsibility."

"Yes, you will be shaping the lives of many kids now."

"Thanks, Tanya, for making me feel even more nervous."

Tanya laughs. "Dad, it is okay. You will be fine. Mom would be proud of you."

Tim pauses for a moment. "Thank you, sweetie. How's school?"

"Hard, real hard, but it is interesting. The courses in psychology is kicking my butt I think more than the marketing and business ones. Math is more difficult just in the way it is done for statistics but I love it."

"I am proud of you and your mom is too looking from above."

Tanya chokes up a little. "Thank you, Daddy. I need to go and visit with some friends but I love you and will see you soon this summer."

"Love you too, honey, and have fun."

They hang up and Tim has a cold drink on the porch and smiles about his prospects.

Tamed Ghosts and New Haunts

After a couple of years, Tim has become well seated in his position and things run smoothly. He heads home but on the way stops at a sandwich shop.

The sandwich maker asks, "Can I help you, sir? Wait a minute. Mr. Jenkins."

"Dane, is that you? You look actually respectable. What happened to you since school?"

"I was kicked out from the old school and it turns out it was probably the best thing because it separated me from my old man. I left, got my GED, and went to community college while I worked as a mechanic. I did a 360 and took management courses and got my associate's degree."

"I was not aware of business courses that are associates."

"Well, it was a course to help people manage stores and so forth. It helped me become a manager here in this chain."

"That is good, Dane, you seem a lot more…calm."

Dane smiled. "I was a punk back in high school, thought I had it all together. The real world definitely changes your attitude about things. Hey, how is Tanya?"

Tim pauses for a moment and says, "She is fine, in college studying marketing."

"That is good, she is a nice girl. I don't know why I was so obsessive about her. I am glad she is doing well."

"Maybe, Dane, why you were so attached to her is she was in a life that you craved. Obviously you were not happy and maybe that is why you were making others unhappy."

"That makes sense. I have a girlfriend and she manages another store. She helped me get into this gig."

"That is great, Dane. Sorry, excuse the pun."

"I have heard that one a few times. Can I ask you a question?"

"Sure."

"Vickie, who was she?"

"She is a unique woman who changed my life in many ways. I hated her at first but sometimes that is the spark that leads to a good friendship."

"She definitely got things over me but it turned out to be the best thing for me too."

"Dane, it is not about Vickie or anyone else, it is about life sometimes knocking you in a different direction to where you should be. The only way to change us sometimes is with a difficult event. People like Vickie are just the catalyst for change because they are so proactive in doing things in life. At least that is the way I see it."

"I can see it and that does make sense to me. Maybe when we get knocked around a time or two we start to look around and figure out where we are supposed to be so we don't have to be knocked next time."

Tim looks astonished "Dane, I think you are going to do well." Dane and Tim shake hands as Tim leaves for home with his food.

Tim spends time in a local bookstore and happens to see the book he gave Lana when they first dated. The manager of the book store notices him looking at the book and says, "One of my favorites."

Tim turns and says, "Yes, it is one of mine too, gave it to my late wife when we first dated."

"I'm sorry, I did not mean to bring that up."

Tim looks up and says, "Oh, no problem, it was years back. I'm Tim Jenkins."

"Nice to meet you, I'm Stacie Thompson, I manage the store here."

"Nice to meet you."

"I have seen you in here a few times. You must love to read."

"I do, it gives me a sense of escape. I guess that is why we all read."

"Of course. You would not happen to be the principal of our high school, are you?"

"Yes, I am. Guess my reputation precedes me."

"It does, it seems. I hear a lot about you."

"Really?"

"In this job you hear a lot of conversations."

"I just bet you do. You know, it is bugging me but haven't we met before?"

"I used to moonlight at carnival town long ago."

"My God, that is where I saw you, I knew it. I used to take my daughter Tanya there. I did not know you worked there, small world."

Stacie smiles. "Yes, it seems."

"So what about you? Married, kids?"

"Divorced, no kids, bounced around away from here and back to finally live here."

"I am divorced too and have a kid that is in her last year of college coming up."

"I am sorry, I thought you said your wife passed away."

"Not explaining things very well, am I? She divorced me but later developed cancer and died."

"My husband was a good man and I really messed up with him. Live and learn, I guess." Stacie is looking down, like in another world.

Tim broke her reverie. "Look, would you like to have dinner with me sometime?"

"I am off Saturdays, would that work?"

"That would be fine. Seven fine?"

"That is perfect. How about I meet you here in the parking lot then?"

"Great, I will see you then."

Stacie smiles. "I will see you then. Okay, I need to get back to the rat killing."

Tim smiles and Stacie walks away to put books away and she keeps looking at Tim once in a while.

Tim arrives Saturday at the bookstore parking lot as Stacie shows up right on time and she pulls up alongside him.

Stacie asks, "Your vehicle or mine or meet you there?"

Tim replies, "I will take you there, if you are comfortable with that."

Stacie says sure. She locks her car and jumps into Tim's. They arrive at a popular quiet seafood restaurant.

Tim asks, "Is this okay?"

"It is fine, I love seafood."

They go in and sit at the booth table. Drinks are ordered and there is silence for a bit, while one of them waits for the moment to break the evening's ice.

Tim goes first. "Have you ever eaten here before?"

Stacie quickly responds, "Oh, yes. I mean, I have before."

Tim smiles and asks, "How do you like the bookstore?"

"It is good, it is a job. Peaceful for the most part."

"What is the nonpeaceful part?"

"Once in a while you get some guy that is a little creepy. I have one now that seems to watch me all the time. I can't really say much I guess to be honest I have been watching you a bit too."

Tim is taken back a little and asks, "That is okay, it is nice to be noticed especially at my age."

"You are not that old."

"Who is this guy that is stalking you?"

"Oh, him? He seems harmless, just catch him looking at me and he walks away. It is flattering really."

"Don't be too sure, you never know about people."

"I appreciate the concern, but I think I am okay. So, tell me about your life? Your wife?"

"I met Lana when we were very young. I actually followed her home and her dad tried to chase me off. Eventually we were married and had a daughter Tanya. Seems like a million years ago and a lot of things happened from that time to now."

"You stalked her, huh?" Tim blushes and begins to respond when Stacie says, "Did not mean to embarrass you, Tim."

"It is quite all right, I am past worrying about things actually. What about you, if you don't mind me prying into your life."

"No, it is fine. I married a guy that I knew from early childhood. Both his family and mine knew we were meant to be together and I guess I did at the time. It seemed okay and I felt the bumps in our marriage were just the usual issues with sharing a life with someone. However, I was unhappy and thought that maybe being with someone else is the answer. I worked at a department store and there was a man that frequented the place and always flirted with me. It was nice to have the attention. We went to have drinks after work and little did I know a friend of my husband's saw us and when I got home my husband already knew. No matter what I said or explained, he would not believe me."

"He had to know that was all but I guess he was not buying into anymore."

Stacie stares like she is weighted down with a burden as she responds chokingly, "Yes, he filed for divorce after he moved out. The fact is, it was not the first time he caught me with someone. The prior one I did have an affair with and he never let me forget it. I was so miserable because he would not forgive me for it. If I had a brain I should have just left him instead of having an affair. But when you are young, you think you can do anything and no one will know. It was not just that but I was miserable over family issues and my brother had died. Bet you are ready for this date to be over?"

"No, not really, and I am sorry about your brother. Everyone has some issue in their life. If there was no forgiveness, there would be no chance to correct ourselves."

"Okay, I spilled my guts all over this nice table, how about we hear about this issue of yours."

Tim looks for a long time as Stacie rests her head on her fists raising her eyebrows at him once in a while. "I stalked my ex-wife Lana and thought about attacking her. I had stalked her for a while but circumstances turned out she liked me and she started dating me. I don't know why I wanted to harm her then, I guess I just saw her as me and I wanted to hurt me."

Stacie looks puzzled as Tim continues, "I was molested as a child and that does not excuse what I did to them. I was really messed up."

"To them? There was more than one?"

Tim looks around and starts getting misty and wiping his forehead as he responds; "My ex was one I tried but failed but later on about eleven years later there was a woman I stalked and tried to harm. However, she overtook me and made me pay for what I tried to do. Bet you are ready to leave now, are you?"

"No, Tim, I am not worried. I don't see harm in your eyes, please continue."

"Thank you for not, well, you know. Anyway, this lady was named Vickie and she turned my life around and made me face the horror I was making. She was instrumental in helping me turn it all around and even saved my daughter from certain fate with a man who kidnapped her."

"Sounds like she was what you needed."

"She was, I owe her a lot. However, it was too late for my marriage as we were both unhappy and I was too wrapped up in myself to recognize she was just playing the part."

"Tim, I think we all play the parts but we have to find happiness in those parts. I learned that too late to practice that belief with anyone else."

"Yeah, well, I learned a lot of things too late. I wish there was something that could have helped deal with the issue as a child and help me be a proper adult. I could have been killed doing the stupid stuff I did, or jail with a near impossible chance to have a good life."

"It is never too late, Tim, for anyone. They may have to pay for their mistakes sometimes with their life but they can change. Sounds like we had some hurdles in our life to jump over."

"Outside of Vickie, I never shared this with anyone, especially someone I just got to know. Thank you for being so understanding."

Stacie smiles. "Tim, you can share anything with me, I won't run off. I am honored you did share it with me. That is a very difficult burden."

"Not really anymore for me. I can talk about it much easier now, I guess it is easier with practice."

"Not practice, it is easier because it is not you anymore. When you truly change, it is like you are remembering someone else's life from before."

"You are on the money. I feel at ease talking to you."

"I like hearing your voice and I am comfortable with you too. Look, I think we have bled ourselves out enough for one evening. Maybe if you would like to see me again you would call me or come by the store?"

"You will see me again soon, and maybe you will still be interested in me, maybe?"

Stacie smiles. "You never know, but I think I would like to see you again."

They finish their meals and he brings her back to her car and makes sure she gets underway.

Sunday, he walks into Stacie's bookstore and sees her working alone behind the counter. She has not noticed him yet as he looks over and a man is intently staring at her. Tim thinks to himself this must be the one she was talking about as he makes his way behind the man. The man is oblivious to Tim's presence as Tim stands directly behind him. The man moves a bit and bumps Tim and excuses himself but Tim is blocking the way. The man stares at Tim as Tim says, "I know what you are up to. You like her but not in a real way, just in a way that is not healthy for both of you. She knows you have been stalking her and you think that you will win her over? Look, go back to your wife and tell her how you feel about things in truthfulness and let the chips fall where they may."

The man asks, "How did you know I am married?"

"You are not wearing a ring but your finger still holds the marks of wearing a ring recently. You took it off when you came in here, didn't you?"

The man looks down and back up at Tim with a wide-eyed look.

Tim continues, "Why don't you leave? You are finished here. However, if you don't want to listen to me, I can introduce you to a nice woman I know."

"You are crazy, mister. Let me go."

"By all means."

The man leaves slowly, looking back at Tim once in a while. Stacie catches the scene as the man leaves the store. She looks over at Tim and smiles and Tim smiles back, walking over to the counter.

"Little help with customer service?"

"Timmy, Timmy, Timmy, what am I going to do with you?"

"Just wanted to see you again."

"I'm glad. We close early, maybe we can visit afterward?"

"I really need to get a couple of things done this evening for school tomorrow but I can wait till you close, you know, just to make sure that man does not come back."

"That is just fine." She continues to work as Tim browses through the books. She locks up the store and Tim walks her to her car.

Tim says, "You know, I really came to tell you that you might want to hold off from seeing me. After sleeping on it I just don't feel I can have a relationship again. I know we just went out one time but things tend to not work out and I just don't want to waste your time. I know I am being stupid but that is the way I feel."

"Fine, Tim, we won't see each other again. Have a good night."

Tim watches her leave as he gets in his car and drives to his home. As he walks slowly to his house feeling bad, he looks over and Stacie is standing there at the end of the yard. He walks over to her and asks, "You followed me here?"

"I stalked you, is that okay? I know you didn't mean what you said. You are just feeling a little guilty and scared. You don't chase me off that easily. The only time you were not honest with me was just now at the store trying to convince me to leave you."

Tim is astonished as he replies, "I don't want to hurt you."

Stacie interjects, "That is why I won't let you go, I know you like me. Give yourself a chance to be happy."

Tim paces around in a circle and says, "I just don't want you to have to bear the cross of my ex."

"Tim, give me a chance to find that out."

"You have a deal. Please come in for a while."

Stacie smiles. "Oh, by the way, I have a present for you." She pulls a book out and gives it to Tim. Tim tears up and looks intently at Stacie as she says, "Let's get this started right."

Tim grabs her and kisses her passionately for what seems like forever. She looks back at him. "Well, Tim, you don't waste time, do you?"

"Time is too valuable to waste, especially when you meet the right person."

She smiles as they go into his house and they spend the evening detailing their entire lives to the late hours. Days pass and very few go by without them seeing each other. One day Tim arrives at her store and brings a paperback to her to buy.

"Ma'am, I would like to buy this book."

Stacie smiles. "Yes, sir. Anything else?" She picks the book up, and the middle of the pages are cut out and a ring falls out of the middle.

"Yes, I would like you to marry me." He kneels down as the entire store seems to halt watching the action. Stacie puts her hand over her mouth and starts crying, gasping for words.

Tim patiently stares up at her as she says quietly, "Yes, yes, I love you." He stands and reaches over to her to kiss as the store claps.

Months later during the summer they have their wedding as family, friends, and coworkers arrive to witness this event. Tanya is the maid of honor as everything proceeds beautifully. They arrive at the reception and Tim introduces Stacie to Vickie.

"This is Vickie, Vickie, Stacie."

Stacie says, "It is so nice to meet you finally. I have heard so much about you."

"I would not have missed this for the world. You two look perfect together, and you have quite a catch here, Stacie."

"I know, the one I should have been with long ago but glad I finally found him."

Tim says, "Thank you for coming, Vickie."

The evening goes on with dancing and cake cutting as Stacie grabs Vickie and brings her over to Tim. Stacie says, "Tim, dance with her please."

Tim blushes as Vickie smiles and they dance.

Tim says, "We have been through a lot, you and I."

"Seems like ages ago we started off on our fun together. But you know, Tim, you helped me a tremendous amount."

"That is what friends do."

They dance and as the music ends they smile and Tim walks to his wife. Vickie stands there with a smile on her face as she starts to have fun with the festivities of the evening. Tanya quiets the room to make a toast as everyone intently listens.

"Dad and mom, I am so happy for you. This is such an emotional moment for me it is hard to talk. I just wanted to say to my dad that you deserve this and I want your life to be wonderful everyday with her. Stacie, welcome to our family." Stacie leaps up and hugs Tanya crying. Tanya calls out, "Vickie, your turn. Speech!"

Vickie smiles and strolls over and says, "Tim and Stacie, this is a union a long time in the making. You went through life's trials and tribulations, honing you to a fine edge so you could both complement each other. Now the time has come and the world has brought you two together to balance everything and give the answer to a lifelong question. Peace and happiness to you both."

Tim, Stacie and Tanya walk over to Vickie and hug her. The evening draws to an end as Tim and Stacie run to their car which is covered with decorations as their family and friends have had fun with their vehicle. They get in the car as Tim finds a book on the car's console. It is the one he gave to Lana long ago. Tim looks at Vickie and smiles pointing at her. Vickie gives a look back with a big smile. They drive off to honeymoon in Hawaii.

The Gift that Keeps on Taking

Tanya has graduated college and works as an intern in Vickie's company. Tim and Stacie has since remodeled Tim's home to make it theirs as Lana's old room has been remodeled by Tanya as her visiting room which keeps some of her mom's things. It is a nice blend of keeping her memory but being comfortable at the same time. Tanya works in the big city with her new job but spends almost each weekend to drop by her dad and stepmom. Stacie and Tanya have grown close, sharing things like a mom and daughter would.

Tim had been helping put Tanya through college with the help of a scholarship from Vickie's company, but begins to realize that between his help, scholarship, and Tanya's part-time job the expenses of college don't add up. He asks Tanya about how she made up the difference in costs compared to what she needs.

"Honey, how did you make up the financial shortfall in college?"

Tanya asks, "What shortfall, Dad?"

"Well, you asked for this amount each semester but your paychecks and scholarship money does not complete the costs that I am seeing here. I asked you if you needed anymore, I would see what I could do."

"It all worked out, I did not want to ask any more from you since you were strapped for cash."

"I appreciate that but where did you get the cash from?"

"Dad, don't worry about it. I can take care of myself."

"I'm sorry, honey, you can take care of yourself. So where did you get the money?"

Quickly, Tanya replies, "Dad!"

Tim smiles and walks away but still confused how she could afford it. That night Tim talks to Stacie about it.

"I am really bothered by how Tanya was able to pay bills with money tapped out."

"Why does this bother you so much?"

"I just don't understand where the money came from and it bothers me."

"Maybe Vickie helped her more than you know."

"I don't think so because Vickie is dealing with the expenses of her own daughter. Just the fact that Tanya won't tell me bothers me."

"Well, she graduated and there is no debt, so maybe you should just let it go."

Tim gives her a kiss and lays down to sleep. The next day after work he drives to the city to talk to Vickie. He is welcomed by Vickie as Tanya walks up and says, "Dad, what are you doing here?"

"I have some things to ask Vickie relating to school. So how is it all here?"

Tanya; "It is fine, Dad, I got to get back to it."

Vickie welcomes Tim in her office as Tim looks around. "Wow, what an office, your own bathroom and everything. This is what it is like at the top?"

"It has its perks for sure. It is good to see you, Tim. What can I do for you today?"

"I just wanted to thank you for helping Tanya in college."

"She earned that scholarship, was not my choice to give it to her."

"No, I mean the extra money with expenses, that was nice of you."

"Not sure I understand, Tim. Are you talking about personal money?"

"Yea..exactly."

"You realize how much a science degree costs? I make good money but it has seriously tapped me. So you are mistaken if you think I helped Tanya, got my own daughter's college to pay."

"You did not give Tanya any money at all?"

"No, Tim. Why, what is the problem?"

"Based on the scholarship funds, what I gave her, and what she earned in her part-time job, she should not have been able to pay for all her college expenses. I just don't understand why she won't tell me how she made it up."

"She is a very smart girl and she obviously found a way, just count your blessings. Look, Tim, she is not a drug dealer."

"I know she is not a drug dealer. It just bothers me how she made up the thousands."

"Look, Tim, I will ask her and if it is something bad I will let you know. If it is something okay, then I will just tell you not to worry about it. Okay?"

"Okay, that is fine. Thank you, Vickie."

Vickie walks Tim out showing him things in the company and telling him what Tanya has been doing as they leave. A couple of days later, Vickie calls Tim at work saying; "Tim, I had a talk with Tanya and was able to pry the information out of her. You have nothing to worry about."

"All right, that makes me feel a little better. Thank you, Vickie. It just bugs me not knowing how she did it."

"Like I said, she is smart about things and can take care of herself."

"Thank you, Vickie."

Vickie says good-bye and hangs up the phone as she looks up at Tanya in her office. She says, "I kept my promise, as you can see."

Tanya says, "I hate keeping it from him. I kept that other thing from him and it ate me up."

"I know it did but it was important. Just like this thing. He considers you his little princess and if he knew you slept with an older guy for money to pay for college, it would crush him."

"I know, and I am not proud of it, but he did not have any more money. I could not stand it if he sold my grandma's home which is what I was afraid he would do."

"I would have helped you myself if I could have but when you told me what you were doing I did not like it and still don't."

"Like I told you, I am not a child anymore and some of my friends have done this to help pay for college. It is hard but having a benefactor to help pay for it is sometimes the only option. College is so expensive."

"I know it is, and I know this kind of thing happens. That is why I only agreed to it if I could find the right guy that is discreet. I know him well and he certainly did not want his family to ever find out what he was doing. We just need to put this behind us now, but you need to find some kind of an excuse to explain how you made that money in case your dad presses you on it."

Tanya looks around. "I know, I know. I will think of something."

"Well, hit the job and we will just let this be."

Tanya nods her head and leaves. That evening, Tim tells Stacie that Vickie gave him the notice that Tanya earned the money legitimately but still bothered, he asks, "I know I am not supposed to worry about it but it is just so much money."

"Tim, just let it go."

"Yeah, but what bothers me is handling her finances through college she made cash deposits of five hundred every few weeks almost on a regular basis and always five hundred cash."

"That is weird, but maybe she was working another job under the table."

"What pays you cash on a regular basis like that and that kind of money?"

"You know what, Tim, why don't you ask her old roommate."

"That is a good idea. I know how to find her."

Tim and Stacie hit the bed as Tim finds renewed hope to relieve what is bothering him. Tim tracks down his daughter's college roommate and good friend but she is reluctant to tell him anything. She only says that Tanya was in sales part time. Frustrated, he asks Stacie if she will find out for him. Stacie calls Vickie and asks her and after a long talk Stacie thanks Vickie and comes home from her job to tell Tim the news. They sit down for dinner as Stacie says, "I know you are sitting on your hands waiting to know what Tanya did for money. I spoke with Vickie and she told me that Tanya sold office toys door to door at businesses. It was not exactly a legit job as she just dealt with cash, but she did well."

"You really believe that? Five hundred in commission every few weeks? I don't buy it."

"I don't know, Tim, that is what Vickie told me."

"I'm sorry, it was wrong to ask you to do that."

"No, honey, it is okay, I want you to be happy."

Tim decided it was not worth it and decided maybe he is just being obsessive.

Tanya was moved to the Marketing Department as an East Coast strategist as a couple of years have moved by and the hard work has paid off. She has met a junior executive of sales in one of her client companies by the name of Sean Stamp. Sean is an upward mobile idealistic young man working his way up the executive ladder. He and Tanya became very close. As the months go by, their love just seems to grow stronger. She finally brings him over to have dinner with her dad and Stacie.

Sean is eating and says, "Mrs. Jenkins, this is a wonderful meal."

Stacie replies, "You are very nice and a good liar, I don't cook that well. But thank you."

Sean smiles at Tanya as Tim asks, "So, Sean, it is nice to finally see you, heard so much about you but need to ask, how do you really like the meatloaf?"

Tanya has a small sigh of relief as she sticks her tongue out at her dad. Tim smiles back at her as Sean replies, "It is very good. Don't get many home-cooked meals as much as I work."

"So you two look happy, it is the happiest I have seen Tanya in a long time."

Sean says, "Well, I think the world about this girl and I had planned to give this to her earlier but now is as good as time as ever." Sean digs in his pocket as he now has everyone's attention and Tanya's eyes are like saucers. Sean puts a ring box on the table in front of Tanya as Stacie covers her mouth, almost crying. Tanya looks down at the box and back up at Sean as she opens it and finds a plastic spider ring in it.

Tanya smirks and laughs as she tells Tim and Stacie, "Well, he always said he was going to win me a spider ring."

They all laugh at the good joke as Sean kneels down and opens up another ring box with a stunning diamond ring. The room is dead silent as Sean asks, "Tanya, I have seen many others but you are the only one I want. Will you spend the rest of your life with me? Will you marry me?"

Crying, Tanya says yes. They hug and kiss each other as they sit back down.

Tanya says, "Wow, I don't know if I can eat. What a surprise, you are so traditional about things I am surprised you did not talk to my dad first for permission."

"He did, sweetie. He took me to lunch last week and asked me."

Tanya looks back at Sean and starts crying. "That is so nice."

Tanya excuses herself, giving Sean a kiss and leaving the room to go to the kitchen with Stacie in tow. As the girls look at the ring, Sean looks at Tim as Tim raises his glass and Sean responds in kind. A few months later, Tanya begins the plans of her wedding which is a few months away itself. She visits her fiancé's company for a lunch together as she enters his office Sean stands up and kisses her and introduces a new executive he is working for now as the new boss. The new boss stands up and both he and Tanya look shocked as Sean says, "Honey, this is Ken Stiles, my new boss. Ken, my fiancé, Tanya." Uncomfortably, they both shake hands as Ken says, "It is nice to meet you, Tanya."

"It is nice to meet you sir."

They seem locked on each other as Sean breaks the gaze, asking Ken if he would excuse them for lunch. Ken replies,

"Certainly. We will catch up later this afternoon. You two have fun and nice to meet you."

Tanya waves back as they leave and Sean asks, "You know him, honey?"

"No, I thought I met him at my company but it must be his twin in life."

Sean accepts the answer as Tanya seemed visibly nervous. After lunch, Sean and Ken meet up and began talking strategies and work flow.

Ken says, "Your fiancé is a nice lady, you are lucky man."

Sean replies, "Thank you, Ken. She thought she knew you from her company but was amazed how much you look like him."

Ken has a good poker face but is very relieved as he replies, "I must have one of those faces."

Sean smiles as they continue with business. The next day, Ken receives a call from a woman named Victoria. As he answers, he recognizes Tanya's voice. "Very smart using your fake name you used in college, but risky don't you think?"

Tanya says, "I only need to know one thing. You are not going to tell Sean about us, are you?"

"I have a wife, kids, and an entire family on both sides of me and my wife's family fence that I don't want to lose. You have nothing to worry about. As far as I am concerned, nothing ever happened."

Tanya is sighing relief, saying, "Okay, I accept that. I never thought in a million years this thing would come back to bite me."

"It hasn't, and maybe you should just think of this as reassurance that the secret is okay. I do have to say I miss you though."

"Look, I am getting married and it is over. It was just to help pay for college."

"I know, but you did not seem to be concerned with marriage when it was mine. How about one more time for old time's sake?"

"Please, let this go."

"I am not threatening Sean's job or your secret from him, I am not that kind of guy. I am just saying I have needs still and that did not end just because you graduated. I do have money, even more now in this new job."

"I don't need money, I work now. Just please let this end."

"One more time, please, and then I will forget about you completely. I'm not that bad looking of a guy."

Tanya pauses. "Look, you are a good looking guy for your age, but please let this go. Maybe you can find another college girl."

"I like you and don't want another. Just one more time and I am good, I promise."

"If I meet you at our usual place one more time, will you let it go?"

"Absolutely, and I will make a substantial wedding present to you on your big day."

"Okay, tomorrow lunch time."

Ken acknowledges as they hang up. Tanya walks up to the apartment that Ken has been renting the whole time they met up through half her college life. She hesitates and finally knocks as Ken answers. "Hi, cutie."

"Please, let's just get this over with."

Tanya walks by him as he closes the door.

The next day at work, Tanya is staring at her desk distracted and feeling guilty. Vickie enters. "Tanya, we need to have a quick meeting. Are you okay?"

Tanya smiles. "Yes, I am okay, this wedding stuff has me overwhelmed."

"Why I never got married, but it looks good on you." Vickie leaves as Tanya prepares for her meeting. Later that evening, having a quiet dinner with Sean, Tanya is still distracted.

Sean asks, "What is wrong, cutie?"

Tanya replies surly, "Don't call me that."

"Sorry."

"I'm sorry, honey, it was a tough day. Anyway, this meal is good."

"The best Chinese in this block."

Tanya smiles and asks, "How is your new boss?"

"He is a cool guy actually. We hit it off well. He comes from a rival company nearby. Poor guy has been through it.

His wife divorced him over a year ago because she thought he was having an affair and got custody of their kids."

Tanya's face is drooping, and she asks, "Divorced? That is so sad."

"Yeah. He confided in me that he was guilty of it and was having an affair with a girl in college. What was even more messed up, he was having an affair with her roommate too." Tanya started choking and said she needed to go to the bathroom. In the bathroom she is throwing up as Sean stands outside asking if she is okay. Tanya simply tells him she is not feeling well and she will be okay. She comes out pale and asks Sean if he would mind cutting it short as he replies, "I already put the leftovers in the fridge and cleaned up. I was just waiting to say goodnight."

Tanya says, "I don't deserve you."

Sean kisses her cheek and says, "Sure you do. Love you, babe."

Tanya tears up as he leaves. The next day, Tanya asks to see Vickie. Vickie says, "Sure, Tanya, what is wrong?"

They sit down at the small conference table in Vickie's office. Tanya starts crying as Vickie asks; "Did Sean do something to you? I will take care of it if he did." Tanya says; "No, it is not Sean. It is his new boss, Ken. You know, Ken, the one you set me up with in college."

Vickie looks stunned. "Ken is Sean's boss, oh my God. Did he notice you?"

"Sean introduced us the other day and we acted like we did not know each other. I called Ken yesterday to make sure we were good and he told me he did not want his wife and kids find out about us but then he asked me for one more time together."

"His wife left him long ago and what did he do when you told him to leave you alone?"

Tanya quickly replies, "I slept with him."

"You what? Look, I recommended him because he was stable with a family but now he has no one."

"Sean knows he slept with a college girl and that he lost his family over it and Sean even told me that he slept with her roommate which was my best friend from high school."

Tanya is crying heavily as Vickie replies, "What a mess, one thing leads to another. I really made a bad situation for you, kiddo. Did you talk to your old friend?"

"Yes, and she admitted to it. She said she followed me to his apartment and arranged to do the same things with him in between times we were together. I trusted her with my secret and she took advantage of it."

"And I take it you are not friends now."

"I never want to know that bitch again. I told her she was a lying bitch and to never talk to me again."

"Hmmm, okay. Well, you know what the problem is now."

"I know. How can I tell Sean what I did?"

"No, the problem is that Ken is going to keep coming back at you. He has no one now so he has nothing to lose."

Tanya gasps. "Oh my God, you think he will ask again?"

"Darling, if it worked one time, it is bound to work again in his mind."

"I am going to be sick."

"Look, I got you into this and I will get you out of it."

"What are you going to do? How can you touch this guy without endangering Sean's job?"

"Trust me."

As the days pass Tanya is a total wreck and Sean is perplexed not knowing how to take care of her. Vickie waits for Tanya to report to her the next time Ken asks to see her again. Finally Tanya gets a phone call from Ken saying, "Hi, Tanya, been thinking about you a lot lately. I am sorry if I seemed forward last time, I do feel bad about it but I helped put you through college and deserve a little credit."

"I knew you would call again, if I meet with you one last time would you please stop bothering me?"

"Absolutely."

"Okay tomorrow lunch see you there."

Tanya hangs up as he continues talking. The next day Ken is at his apartment waiting when the door bell rings. He opens the door and Vickie is standing there. "Vickie, nice to see you, what are you doing here?"

"Ken, let me in, we need to talk." They adjourn to the room and sit down.

"Ken, I know I set you up with Tanya in college because I knew you and you were a good man. I knew you did not screw around and were stable. Now, however, you got caught cheating with Tanya's roommate by your wife and that ended your marriage, lost custody of your kids, and even your job. I know all about it and I am here to say I am sorry about all of it. But I cannot let you take advantage of Tanya in this way. Do you understand me?"

Ken looks around. "I did not want to do this but I am alone and I have needs." Ken gets up and starts walking around as he continues, "I really messed it all up for myself. What the hell was I thinking? Me, a middle-aged man with a college girl, I had no business with that. My marriage was dull but that was not my ex-wife's fault. It was no one's fault, it just happened. I guess I just could not accept the fact I am getting old and women are not interested in me anymore. I feel so stupid and ashamed." He sits down and puts his face in his hands.

Vickie says, "Look, Ken, I know you are not a bad guy, I have known you for years. I am sorry you got caught up in this midlife crises and I took advantage of you to fulfill the financial needs of Tanya. But you need to leave this alone and move on with your life. Tanya is so in love with Sean and this could destroy them."

Ken stares at Vickie and walks to the window as he turns. "You're right, I will leave her alone. Sean has nothing to worry about in his job as well. I just need to get my life together and move on like you say."

"That is the Ken I know. I am going to leave now. You going to be okay?"

"You know, I think I will be just fine. I actually feel okay."

"See you later, Ken." Vickie leaves as she calls Tanya to tell her the news. Tanya is relieved believing it is over. Days later she has not heard from Sean and that evening she goes to Sean's apartment. Sean visibly is not happy to see her but invites her in.

"What is wrong Sean?"

"I had a visit at my office by a woman named Sarah. She said she was your college roommate and had an affair with my new boss Ken. She told me that she met Ken because he was paying you for sex. I thought this was all crazy till Ken walked in the office and it was obvious they knew each other despite Ken trying to deny it all. That time you first met Ken, you did know him, didn't you?"

Tanya is crying. "Yes, it is all true. I am so sorry, I can't believe how worthless I am."

"I'm hurt, I'm hurt because you did not tell me the truth."

"I should have told you everything. I slept with Ken after we met at your office. He told me it would be the last time but then kept asking till Vickie convinced him to back off.

There is no forgiving me over this." She pulls her engagement ring off and hands it to him as tears roll off her face.

Sean picks up the ring and says, "I know about you and Ken. After I kicked Sarah out, Ken came clean with me and apologized. Sarah was there because Ken had still been seeing her off and on since college and cut her off when all this went down. She came to my office to get back at you because she blamed you for Ken cutting her off."

"My God."

Sean grabs her hand and says, "You made mistakes, but that does not make you any less of a person." Sean slides the ring back on her finger and says, "Let's start over. Will you marry me?"

Astonished and crying harder, Tanya hugs Sean and says, "Yes, forever."

Tanya and Sean

Months pass and the wedding is beautiful with Vickie as the maid of honor. At the reception, Tim walks up to Vickie. "Always a bridesmaid but never a bride."

Vickie says, "Ha-ha, very funny Tim. It is a beautiful wedding, Tim."

"It is nice but I can't take credit for it. Sean's boss Ken paid for it all."

"He is a good guy. You know he himself has a new girlfriend, he must be feeling generous."

"Apparently so."

Sean walks up to Ken. "Thank you, Ken, for the wedding and the promotion."

Ken replies, "It is my honor. Thank you for making me your best man. Your parents would be very proud to see the man you are if they had lived."

"They are with me always. Come on, have a dance with the bride."

"I don't feel that is appropriate."

"Nonsense, Tanya insisted."

At that moment Tanya walks up as she grabs Ken by the arm and pulls him to the dance floor. He is quiet as Tanya says, "Thank you for the beautiful wedding."

"I am sorry for everything, it is the least I could do."

"Don't be sorry, we were all actors in a bad play."

The music ends and Tanya kisses Ken on the cheek as she walks up to her husband. Ken's girlfriend Tammy walks up and grabs him. "You okay, Kenny?"

"Perfect," he replies.

The reception draws to a close as a new happy couple leaves. The people start leaving as Tim just stares the direction of the car his daughter left in. Stacie tells Tim, "I will be inside helping with the cleanup."

Tim smiles as he thinks about the time his daughter first took her steps, to the time she was kidnapped, and the times he helped her with school, to graduation from college, and now married. The memories wash over him like a waterfall as he tears up and is happy that things have worked out. Looking up at the night sky and the starry night, he whispers, "Thank you, Lord, for everything." He returns to the hall to help with cleaning.

History Repeats

After some time, Tanya and Sean formed her own marketing company with the help of Vickie and Ken. Ken had remarried but after a couple of years died in a car accident. Tanya and all who knew Ken attended his funeral. Tanya gives a rose to Ken's widow, Tammy. As Tanya looks up, she sees a woman in black standing far away and recognizes it is her old college friend Sarah. Sarah notices that Tanya sees her and Sarah leaves. At work, Tanya puts a picture of Ken up on the conference room wall. Tanya and Sean have dinner with Tim and Stacie.

Tanya says, "Dad, Mom, something interesting happened today." They look puzzled and ask what it is. Tanya continues, "Found out you guys are going to be grandparents."

They laugh and hug Sean and Tanya with happiness. Tanya and Sean have a beautiful little girl they name Victoria. Tanya always liked that name. As the weeks pass, their little girl just seems to get funnier as time goes on. They drop Victoria off at Tim's and Stacie's to babysit so Tanya and Sean can have a date night. Tim has turned Lana's and Tanya's old room into a nursery as it seemed so appropriate. Little Victoria drifts off to sleep as the proud grandparents go downstairs to talk.

Stacie asks, "Tim, does it seem like time gets faster as you get older?"

Tim replies, "It sure does. Seems like yesterday I was changing diapers on Tanya."

"How does this remote baby camera work anyway."

"It is already working, just look at the screen."

"There is no screen, it is dark."

Suddenly they hear a baby screaming and they run upstairs as fast they can go at their age. Running into the room Victoria is gone and the window is open seeing a car driving off.

Stacie screams, "Victoria!"

Tim runs down to his car and drives after the direction of the car but has lost it. He calls Stacie. "I can't find the car."

"I called 911 and they are sending police. I will call Tanya."

Stacie calls Tanya as Tanya and Sean leave the movies to come back to her parent's house. Sean drops Tanya off and joins the hunt for little Victoria. Police arrive at Tim's house and Stacie tells them what happened. The police tell

Stacie and Tanya that the kidnapper threw a towel on the baby camera. Stacie describes the car as police dispatch units to search. The officer asks Tanya if she knows anyone that might want to take her baby.

"No one. Wait." Tanya asks Stacie for her keys and Tanya runs to her car to leave. The officer asks where she is going. Stacie says she does not know but calls Tim and Sean to let him know Tanya left. Tanya drives crying and mad as after twenty minutes she pulls into the apartment complex of her old college roommate Sarah. As she approaches the building Sarah calls down to her from Sarah's third floor apartment balcony while holding Victoria.

"Please don't hurt my baby!"

Sarah says, "You ruined my life, I wanted to be with Ken and now you get a beautiful wedding, your own business while I live as a case worker making nothing."

Police begin to arrive as Tanya yells, "Please, it is not Victoria's fault."

"Victoria, Victoria! You named her your fake whore name with Ken?"

"It is my mother's middle name, I always thought I would name my child that name if I had a girl. I don't know why I used it for Ken, I was nervous and scared. It was a name I knew I would not forget."

Police arrive and begin moving up the stairwell to the apartment. Tanya knows she is running out of time, saying,

"Sarah, you were my best friend through high school, we shared everything. I was hurt that you did what you did with Ken but mostly that you kept it from me. Please don't hurt my baby. I am asking you as you're my closest friend."

Sarah stares at Victoria and back at Tanya.

Tanya looks up, whispering to herself, "Please, Sarah, please."

Sarah slowly puts Victoria down on the balcony. The police ask Sarah to open the front door and give up. Sarah looks at the front door to her apartment and back at Tanya and smiles, leaping off the balcony onto the pavement below, dying instantly. Tanya turns away crying. As soon as the impact happens she runs up the stairs. Police kick the door in and as Tanya reaches the apartment. They hand Victoria to her. Tanya hugs Victoria as the crying baby is being comforted. Tanya reaches the bottom of the stairs as Sean pulls up and gives them a hug. They go back to Tim's and Stacie's as the reunion is emotional and grateful.

Confessions

Days pass as Tanya and Sean have taken some time off and visit with Tim and Stacie since the kidnapping.

Tim says, "I am so sorry for not looking after Victoria."

Tanya stops him and says, "Dad, you did nothing wrong. Sarah had been stalking us. We found out. She was upset at me."

"I can't tell you how it felt losing you long ago and then her."

Sean says, "It is all right, we are just glad to all be back together. No one did anything wrong except Sarah."

The room is quiet for a bit and Stacie asks, "Why was she upset at you, Tanya?"

Tanya and Sean look at each other and Sean says, "They had some fights about personal things, you know."

Tim's ears perk up. "She was not upset about money during college, was she?"

Tanya says, "Dad, please, don't get into this again."

Tim stares and says, "You're right, I don't need to know. You have been through enough."

Tanya looks at the floor and up at Sean and says, "I should just tell him."

Sean takes a deep breath and nods his head. Tanya begins to tell the whole story about how she made extra money in college with Ken and how Sarah got involved and why she was upset. After the explanation, Tim stood up and looked around the room and picked up an old picture of Lana and Tanya together.

Tim finally says, "It hurts, I won't lie. I tried to protect you all these years and was so worried someone would take you like when you were a kid and now I understand you prostituted yourself out to an older man. I wished you would have just told me you needed more money, I would have got it somehow."

"I could not do that, Dad. You were broke and the only thing left would have been to sell this house and I would have dropped out of college before that happened."

Tim looks at Stacie then back and Tanya and says, "You did what you felt you had to do and I know it must had been hard to do and live with. You see the consequences of certain actions. But I love you and that will never change."

"Thank you, Dad. I love you too."

The room is quiet again while Tim looks up and says, "I need to confess something too. When you were eight you remember the first time Vickie came around?"

Tanya nods yes.

"She was not someone whose wallet I found and tried to return it and then got beaten up by a gang later. She beat me up that night."

Tanya gasps. "What?"

Tim starts to choke up and says, "I followed her to her home and tried to rape her. She beat me down hard and started stalking me to make my life miserable. And she did very well in making my life terrible. But in the process she made me realize why I was doing the things I was doing and the lie I was living within myself. She also brought about the lie that your mom and I were living too. I think that ultimately I wanted to be caught and my life crumbled from the normalcy it showed. It was only after your mom and I divorced and I hit rock bottom did I start living truthfully."

Tanya and Sean are stunned, as Tanya asks Stacie, "Did you know about this?"

Stacie answers, "Yes, Tanya, he told me just before we were married. I even talked to Vickie about it at length."

Tanya says, "I understand why you did not tell me, Dad, but this is big."

Tim says, "I know, and I don't expect you to forgive me. But since we are baring our souls I thought you should know. You are old enough and deserve to know."

"I don't know how Sean feels but there is nothing to forgive. You are my dad and obviously Vickie forgave you since she is your friend and she is the only one that really can forgive you."

"She is, and she did, but you are my daughter and I am proud of you. Thank you for understanding me and the fact that I am not the same person, I am not afraid to admit it."

Tanya and Tim get up and hug each other. Sean stands up and hugs Tim, saying, "Dad, you have nothing to worry about from me." Stacie looks on with happiness as the evening ends more festive.

Tanya has lunch a few days later with Vickie to let her know that she knows all about what her dad tried to do.

Vickie says, "I knew this day would come where he would admit it to you. When it happened I got the better of him but even when he threatened me he looked frightened, like he wasn't sure of what he got himself into. At least it seemed that way, but I defended myself in the best way possible. When I got him down I thought of ending his life but something in me wanted to get back at him. I guess I never had the chance to get back at someone who hurt me much earlier so I took it all out on your dad. Despite the vengeance, which some of it felt good, by the way, it did not make me feel better. If anything, I felt like the bad person. I was no longer the victim but the predator. I also realized that he was like me, a victim of abuse, but he let it mess him up to the point of acting it out. He eventually showed himself to me and I had a hard time exacting my revenge. And when he found my daughter and brought her to me, the hate simply disappeared. Not just the hate for him but my hate for everything. The void in myself was filled gaining my daughter back. Your dad is a good man, he was a victim of a horrible event that consumed him and he never learned how to express it correctly. He grew up but the feelings did not. He wanted to hurt someone else like he was hurting. That is no longer true for him anymore."

"I wonder how many people are out there like that. A time bomb waiting to go off."

"As long as they are alone with their feelings and no one to talk it out, a lot."

"Wow, I knew of a few people like that in college and even high school. Loners, no friends or few. Always watching everyone but never engaging anyone."

"We had them too in my day. I was sort of one myself. Having an alcoholic dad made me second guess myself a lot. I was actually pretty shy in school."

"That is hard to believe."

"Well, believe it, I was."

They pause for a moment and Tanya asks, "Vickie, why did you never marry?"

Vickie looks around. "Well, kiddo, I did have a boyfriend in college and he was a great guy. We were actually pretty serious about each other. He was killed by a drunk driver."

"I am so sorry to bring it up."

"It is okay, Tanya."

"What happened to the drunk?"

"Oh, he survived just fine. But after he got past his court battles and his life back, I spent some time with him."

"Oh, Lord, did you 'Vickie' all over him?"

"Let's just say I am his AA sponsor now and he is gladly off the sauce."

"That was it for you, no one else?"

"There was one other guy after I settled in my job and career. He was nice and a good man. We went together for a while but I never got serious about him and he was looking for someone to be serious with. He broke up eventually with me and married a nice lady in our company a couple of years later."

"He was not mister right?"

"He might have been, or at least mister compatible. I got a little distracted at that time because that was when I met your dad."

"Oh my God, it was then? Does my dad know he messed up your relationship?"

"No, and don't tell him please. It is okay, I wasn't really ready to commit to anything yet anyway."

"This man, how serious was he?"

"Pretty serious, he asked me to marry him once. I told him I was not ready to answer it. He was pretty hurt by it because he took a big chance not knowing for sure how I would answer. He told me to hold the ring and let him know. I looked at it once in a while and thought about it. My head was a little swirling about the thought of getting hitched that I went to the bookstore and that was the day your dad followed me home."

"Oh, wow. What did you tell this guy after that?"

"After I had dealt with your dad and his life for a week, I told him I would not marry him. My reasons were that my life had suddenly got really complicated and it was not a good time to do this. He was visibly hurt but told me to keep the ring as a friend's present. I still have it and look at it once in a while. I did go to their wedding and bought them an expensive gift that more than paid for the ring."

"That was fair, but so sad. That is so sad."

"Yeah, but life is full of disappointments but full of new dawns too."

"You are an incredible lady."

"You are nice. I am just an average woman that learned to persevere through tough times." Their lunch ends as they return to work.

Patterns of the Father

Vickie has lunch with the man who wanted to marry her that she was talking to Tanya about, John Patterson.

"Hi, John, nice to see you after all these years."

"Vickie, you look as lovely as ever. How are things since I left the company?"

"They are good, I am now CEO and president of it."

"I knew you would go far."

"How is Angie?"

"We divorced a year ago, just did not work out. But she is good, we still keep up with each other."

"I am sorry to hear about that and this was really awkward asking you to lunch."

"No, no, no, it is fine. I have been wanting to catch up with you for a long time now but just never had the bravery to look you up and ask."

"Well, a lot has happened since you and I were together, a lifetime, it seems."

"Same here, I have a good sponsor in AA that has been with me ever since. Still sober after all these years."

"I am proud of you, John, that is so good."

John looks at her gazing and asks, "Can I ask you what made your life so complicated when we broke up?"

"The day you proposed I went home and was attacked by a would-be rapist. I got him down instead and spent an enormous amount of time being an avenging angel on him. After a time he changed and became a good man. However, I could not think of getting married during that time."

"Well, that makes me feel a whole lot better that it was not me."

"There was nothing wrong with you, you were just fine, actually."

"You know, you seem to have a good effect on bad people. You did me."

"You reminded me of my dad, but you were able to stop drinking especially after the accident."

"I still think of him after all these years. I still think how stupid I was coming over drunk and asking you to choose me over him like you would at that moment. I was just so jealous and immature and felt like he had stolen you away from me. And when you told me to go and was calling him to come over, I left in a rage. I don't remember much after that but remember you at my bedside at the hospital."

Vickie is crying. "I loved you, John, but your drinking was too much. I think I used your friend to try to get you to stop but I started having feelings for him too, as you know. After the accident, I felt I had caused this whole issue and owed it to you to help you. Help you get sober, graduate college, and get a job at my company so I could watch you."

"That you did, and did well. That is why after all those years of friendship I finally had the guts to ask you to marry me. No one ever kept me going as you did, not even Angie could. She tried, God bless her, but she wasn't you. The subject came up frequently and eventually was the reason she left. My heart and mind was on you always. I think now that when you were attacked that day you were just looking for a reason to tell me no but your heart would not. Maybe you were scared."

"I think you are right. I was scared, scared if I married you I would be marrying my dad. You would fall off the wagon and start drinking again. The fact is I loved you and always had."

"I never stopped loving you. I do love you."

"I love you too, John, but so much time has passed."

"Nonsense, love is timeless. But maybe there is too much water under the bridge. Can we remain friends?"

Vickie swirls her straw and smiles.

"Well, I need to go back. I hope to see you soon?" John asks.

John gets up to leave as Vickie calls him, "John." She pulls his ring box and ring out of her purse and opens it. John stares at her intensely, almost perplexed. Vickie says, "Give me some time, will you wait for me a bit?"

John smiles. "I will wait as long as it takes."

Vickie gets up and hugs him. "Thank you, John."

John smiles and leaves. Vickie gets a call from Tanya asking her if she would like to have dinner at her dad's this weekend. "I would love to. Oh, Tanya can I tell you something?"

"Sure what is it."

"I lied the other day about my boyfriend getting killed by a drunk driver, well sort of. He was a boyfriend but not the one I was in love with. The one I loved actually was the drunk driver. He is one and the same guy that proposed to me later."

"Holy cow, life is so strange. You didn't have to confess to me about it, I understand."

"No, I did, because I had lunch with him, his name is John. He is divorced and still in love with me."

"Oh, wow, and how do you feel?"

"I love him but I feel things are still too complicated."

"Only if you make it complicated, Vickie, that is what you told me at one time. We sabotage ourselves with our own excuses."

"How did you get so smart, kiddo?"

"I had a great tutor. See you Saturday at five?"

"I will be there."

Saturday arrives and Vickie shows up with John.

Tanya says, "Vickie! I am so glad you came."

Vickie says, "This is my friend John."

"Nice to meet you, John."

They come in the house and are greeted by Sean, Tim, and Stacie as Vickie makes the introductions. They sit down as Tanya speaks, "So, John, how do you know Vickie?"

"Well, that is an interesting story but the short of it is we went to college together and worked together also."

"So you guys have known each other for quite a while?" Tim asks.

"Yes, we dated off and on."

"And now?"

John and Vickie look at each other as Vickie replies, "We will see, we are good friends."

Stacie prods, "Come on, Vickie, tell all."

"We were engaged to be engaged at one time but we broke up but have always been good friends. John was married and now divorced."

Stacie says, "Okay, you secret agents, that is good enough for now."

Everyone smiles as the room is a little more comfortable but still edgy.

Tanya says, "Well, Sean and I have an announcement, we're pregnant."

Sean says, "Well, I think she will be bearing most of that part though."

Everyone erupts with congratulations and hugs. Everyone begins to pair off to have small conversations as Tim and John take a walk outside.

Tim says, "Vickie looks happy."

John replies, "Thanks, Tim, I feel happy around her."

"So you were engaged in college?"

"No, we really were not engaged. I asked but she had to think about it, that was later on where we worked together about eighteen years ago." Tim stops and John asks, "Something wrong?"

"You say around eighteen years ago?"

"Yeah, thereabouts."

"Why did you guys break up?"

"I wanted to get married but she had some things happen in her life that distracted her."

"What things?"

"I don't think I should get into it because they are personal to Vickie."

"I understand." They walk away quietly as Tim says, "You know she was attacked by a rapist around that time."

"Well, between you and I and a fence post, that was what broke us up. She was so upset that she could not focus on us anymore. I figured it had to do with me and ended up marrying another lady later."

"Did she ever tell you what happened to the rapist?"

"Yes, she said she helped him and they became good friends eventually." They keep walking and John asks, "You're that friend, aren't you?"

"Yes. I am sorry that what I did ruined your lives."

John is quiet as they keep walking.

Tim asks, "You all right?"

"No, not really. How am I to take it knowing I am standing next to the man that tried to rape the woman I love and halted our getting together?"

"I did a lot of damage, I know, John. I am truly sorry for it but if I could take it back I would."

"That is convenient now. If you were a real man you would leave Vickie alone completely and give me the chance to try to have a life again with her."

"I am not in your way at all. If you want me to back away I surely will."

John points his finger. "I am going to leave now because I am getting upset. Just stay away from us, okay?"

"Done."

John walks away back to house and tells Vickie he is not feeling well so they say their good-byes and leave. Vickie looks at Tim as they drive by him. Vickie asks John, "Are you okay?"

"Just fine, not feeling too good right now."

The ride is quiet as they go home.

Some Things Never Change

Weeks pass as Vickie visits with Tim at his house. They adjourn to the study, leaving Stacie alone. Vickie asks, "What did you tell John? He has been upset and distant since the evening you two had your little walk."

Tim answered, "It was nothing, we just talked about sports."

"BS. Be honest with me, Tim."

Tim stares for a bit. "Okay. He told me you guys were serious but you had an incident happen eighteen years ago. I put two and two together and he admitted to me about the rape incident. He then figured out from my expressions I was the rapist. After that he was upset and angry at me. I tried apologizing and told him I was not in his way at all. He told me to leave you two alone and left."

"Well, he and no one gets to dictate who my friends are and how I spend time with them."

"Look, Vickie, if you guys were serious then don't spoil it on the account of me, it is just history repeating itself."

"No, Tim, it is not. This is the reason we had a problem in college because he is so jealous. He is my father all over again."

"I don't know what to say but I am sorry."

"Don't be. I am going to leave now."

"You okay, Vickie?"

"Never better."

Vickie leaves and says good-bye to Stacie as she walks out the door.

The next day, Vickie goes over to John's house. "Hi, Vickie. Sorry I have been a bastard lately, had a lot on my mind."

"You have been stewing about Tim, I know."

"So he told you, I knew he would get between us if he could."

"He is not in between anyone, John. It is your jealousy. You ever heard of the sand principle?"

"No, what is that?"

"The principle is if you have sand you want to keep you hold it in your hand gently. If you try to squeeze it tight and hold it too hard it just slips out of your fingers."

"That is a nice metaphor, so are you slipping out of my hands is what you are saying?"

"Yes, John. Because if you are this paranoid and jealous now, just imagine how it would be if we were married."

"I knew you loved me." He grabs her and kisses her.

"John, Goddamn it, what are you doing? And you are drinking, aren't you?"

"Just a little to calm my nerves."

Vickie walks over to his refrigerator and sees a note with his AA sponsor's number and starts dialing it. John asks, "What are you doing?" Vickie ignores him and tells his sponsor he needs to come over because John is drinking again. The sponsor says he will be right over.

Vickie says, "John, don't let this bring you down. Understand I am not here on this planet to keep you together as some humpty dumpty. You must take care of yourself."

"I love you."

"Love is important, John, but not enough to have a relationship. There has to be respect, honesty, and both parties have to care for themselves. That is the only way they can take care of each other."

"I know I need help, I just need the right woman."

"John, Angie was the right woman. You just did not give her a chance."

The door knocks as Vickie lets the sponsor in. Vickie reaches in her purse and gets the ring box he gave her long ago. "John, what you need I cannot provide for you. Till you understand that, I am actually in the way of your life getting better."

Vickie throws the ring box to him and leaves.

What You Leave Behind

Vickie has settled back into her routine as the weeks pass. She seems bothered a little though, like something is in the air, but progresses through meetings about marketing new items. One day she is visited by Detective Sandberg who works cold cases.

Det. Sandberg says, "Miss Newsome, thank you for seeing me."

"Please call me Vickie. What can I do for you?"

"Well, Vickie, I am working a case involving a Tim Jenkins about sixteen years ago where his daughter was kidnapped but the kidnapper was found beaten to death." The detective is watching Vickie's body movements and pupils to see if any change but Vickie offers no physical tells. "Anyway, this case has gone cold for a while and my job is to put it to resolution. I know you were interviewed by detectives and told them that you never saw Mister Jenkins but he claimed he went to your house."

"I guess so. It was a long time ago."

"I understand it was years back, but one of your neighbors recently remembered seeing Mister Jenkins at your house on that day. She has seen him over your house frequently but specifically remembers him visiting you and was quite agitated. So the question is why would you tell the detectives you did not see him when you did?"

Vickie pauses for a bit and smiles. "Are you sure Mrs. Henderson remembers that day long ago correctly? She is quite elderly."

"Oh, I think her memory is clear because it corroborates with DNA evidence found that was not tested for back then. You see, the hairs found at the scene were blonde and Mr. Jenkins has brown hair. Would you be willing to submit some DNA samples for comparison?"

"At this time you will need to speak to my lawyer."

"Vickie, do we really need to lawyer up? You don't have anything to hide, do you?"

"It is not about hiding anything, it is about protecting myself from your accusations. You can talk to my lawyer."

"Have it your way, Miss Newsome. You will be hearing from me soon."

Detective Sandberg leaves and Vickie calls her lawyer, Guy Jones. She sets up an appointment to see him that day but then calls her daughter Veronica.

"Veronica, how are you doing?"

"Good, Mom. Why are you calling?"

"Just wanted to hear your voice."

"What is wrong? You don't sound too good."

"I am fine, just busy with work. Anyway, let me let you go."

"Okay, Mom, love you."

"Love you too."

Vickie ponders the circumstances while she waits for her appointment. Upon arriving at her lawyer's office, Attorney Jones welcomes her, saying, "Vickie, it is so nice to see you again."

"Hi, Guy, I just love saying that."

"Very funny, only hear that ten times a day. So what is on your mind?"

"I had a detective named Sandberg come to my office basically accusing me for the death of a pedophile that kidnapped a friend's daughter many years ago. The death was blamed on my friend Tim, the father of the kidnapped child, but Tim when questioned at that time said he went to my house that day, not the kidnapper's. The detectives at the time called me and asked me if that was true. I told them no."

"Was it true?" Vickie pauses while Guy responds, "Be honest with me so I can assess the damage."

"Okay, he did. At the time he was not my friend but my nemesis and I wanted him to take the heat for it."

"Why would you want him to take the heat for murder? What did he do to you?"

"Not going into that, it is not relevant."

"It might be in court. Look, if you did not do it, then you are only guilty of lying to the police. You did not do it, right?"

"The detective today said he found blonde hair and other evidence they did not test back then for but wanted my DNA to rule me out."

"Will they rule you out?"

Vickie stares for a long time intently. "No."

"Oh crap. What else do they have?"

"They have testimony of my neighbor that put Tim at my house that day like he claimed."

"After Tim left your house, what did you do?"

"I called a number that lets you know about known registered sex offenders and found three in Tim's neighborhood. I had been watching Tim some and when I went to one of the offender's homes, I recognized the car in the driveway and approached the house. The man answered and I tried to get him to invite me in. I heard Tanya, that's Tim's daughter, whimpering in the bedroom, I burst in.

Went straight to the sounds and there she was tied up and blindfolded. I was furious and in rage at that moment. That predator got into it with me and I…I beat him to death."

Guy says, "Go on."

"I knew I could not stay because I would be in the gas chamber later. I told Tanya she would be safe and not tell anyone. I left and called the police from a payphone. When Tim and his late wife Lana picked up Tanya, the police questioned him. That is when he tried to set his alibi that he was at my house. I told the detectives he was not at my house to put the blame on him. I knew they had no evidence he was there and he would be dismissed."

"Wow, okay, hmmm. Okay, let me take this in for a moment."

Vickie watches Guy pace the room for a bit holding his finger to his mouth. Finally he points it at Vickie and asks, "You are going to have to tell me why you wanted to get back at Tim."

"I can't because he is my friend and his daughter is like my daughter."

"Look, Vickie, you are looking at twenty-five to life and homicides do not go away, there is no statutory expiration for them. I need to know what drove you to do this. If Tim did something wrong, it helps your case."

"I need to think on it."

"Okay, but let me know ASAP, okay?"

"All right."

Vickie leaves his office and makes the drive to Tim after calling him to check if he would be home. She arrives at Tim's to confer about what has happened. After explaining the day, Tim looks around and says, "You got to tell your attorney everything."

"But if I do that and I go to court, what you did will be public. You will lose your job, friends, everything you spent time building up."

"I can't let you go down for this. You saved my daughter and me. I will be fine. I don't care about the consequences."

"I could always tell them it was not an attempted rape but a road rage."

"It won't work because others know and if they slip up then they are in trouble. I do not want people putting themselves at risk for what I did. You need to tell them what happened, it is the only way to justify what you did."

Vickie looks around. "You know, it is funny, at one time I wanted you to go down for this or at least feel the heat of it, now I can't stand the idea of you being blamed for the things you didn't do."

"Do what you need to do to get out of this. I will testify on your behalf, of course."

"Thank you, Tim."

They hug and say their good-byes. Vickie calls her attorney and explains what happened between Tim and her long ago. Guy tells her that he will prepare for a defense if charges are brought to her. A month goes by and all seems quiet at her home when Vickie hears a knock at her door. She answers and it is Detective Sandberg with several uniformed officers.

Sandberg says, "Vickie Newsome, you are under arrest for the charge of murder of Zane Thompson…"

The detective's voice sounds muffled as the police handcuff her till she hears Sandberg say, "Do you understand your rights as they have been told to you?"

Vickie shakes her head yes as she tears up and is escorted out of her home to the police car. Neighbors watch through windows as she is seated in the car. An evidence team walks into her house as the police car takes her to jail. At the jail, she is processed and given the opportunity to call her lawyer then is placed in a holding cell with four other women. One of those women looks at her friend and smiles as she gets up and talks to Vickie.

"Hey, blondie, you want to party?"

Vickie ignores her, looking at the ground.

The woman persists, kicking Vickie's foot. "Hey, bitch, I am talking to you."

Vickie stands up and stares at the woman and says, "Listen, fatso, if I wanted to party, it would not be with you, but if you like I can kick the shit out of you all over this cell."

Silence goes on as the staring continues when the woman says, "Whatever, bitch," as she walks off. Vickie sits down and stares at the door. Vickie is brought out as her lawyer has made bail for her and as she is released.

Guy asks, "Had any problems in there?"

"Nothing I could not handle."

Vickie comes home to find that her house has been completely gone through as she cleans up. The next day she meets with her lawyer.

"Look, Vickie, they have your DNA and hair fibers at the crime scene. They have you lying about Tim and they are going to question Tanya. You need to plea deal with them, take your chances."

"I want to fight this, not deal myself away."

"Look, you might just get some jail time and probation if you deal, otherwise they are going for capital murder."

"You really think they are going to sentence me to death over a stupid pedophile caught in the act?"

"No, not really, but you could face serious time."

"I am not dealing. We are going to fight it."

"Okay, I am going to need to depose you at length about Tim and everything."

"Fine."

Vickie is interviewed by Guy over the next couple of days and going over details of events as well as Tanya and Tim.

It Is Not an Exact Science

Veronica comes to Vickie's home to be by her side and speak about her upcoming trial.

"Mom, I came as fast I could but was tied with the usual grant fundraising, you know, the exciting part of being a scientist."

"It is good to see you. So tell me, how much time do you have to spend finding money to fund your salary?"

"Well, it takes a lot of money to run experiments and often in the field I am in it is considered soft science, not that practical. I have not been in it very long but have already moved around a couple of times. But I spend about 70 percent of my time writing grants. There always seems to be a cutback somewhere so it is hard. You have to stay published quite a bit as well and what you write gets peer reviewed and often criticized hard, especially if what you are trying to prove or say contradicts what others are trying to get funded for."

"Sounds like musical chairs."

"Not quite, but it can feel like it sometimes. It is very stressful, sometimes overwhelming. I tend to bury myself in a paper to keep from thinking about it sometimes. I mean, I love my career, but I thought it was going to be more science and not fundraising. I called you one time when I realized what I would be working on. Just hearing your voice helped me but I was depressed all night. After all that school and postgraduate work, and this was the reward? I got maybe two nights of actual telescope time so far and that was working someone else's project. It is a huge waste of time and talent to have to do administrative work."

"Well, there is a lot of administration work no matter what you do, even if you were a policeman. But in a corporate setting, we have people who specialize in trying to get money and people who do other jobs only have to deal with their job."

"Not in the science world, you do it all. People with money want to hear from the people who will be using it."

"Inefficient, if that were a company it would have folded. Someone needs to rethink how to better utilize our science resources. At least they are not burning you at the stake for heresy, you know."

"I feel like my peers do that enough. Maybe you could change the system someday, Mom. You would be good at it. Anyway, enough about my woes, what is going on with you?"

Vickie looks around and pauses for a moment to smile. "Sweetie, your mom is in a whole lot of trouble. You know from the phone conversation what I am up against. It just does me a lot of good seeing you here."

"How do they think you killed this man?"

"I did."

Veronica starts crying, "What?"

"It was self-defense. I was going to call the police and rescue Tanya. But that man came at me to hurt me and I lost it. I beat him to death. Then I realized it was too late to call the police, they would never believe me. So I told Tanya it was me and she is safe but to be patient because the police are coming. I then called them from a payphone. I later pinned it on Tim because I knew they would never prosecute him."

"Oh wow, this was when you were after Mr. Jenkins."

"That is right. Do you forgive me?"

"Of course I do, you saved Tanya. Just like you did me and Tim. If you had not had taken that predator out, he would just have gotten out and killed the next kid. What you did was wrong, but who can blame you especially defending yourself. I love you, Mom."

"I love you too, dear, but it is not that simple. Lawyers have a way of diluting plain truth to fit their agenda."

They hold each other as they both think of the issues they must face. The next day, Veronica comes in with a box, saying, "Look, Mom, I got some red ribbons to make support ribbons for your court date. But instead of it hanging down they go upside down to show a V for Vickie and Victory."

"That is sweet. I have an appointment with my attorney to talk about the defense."

"What does he think?"

"He is not exactly positive about it. He seems to think there is a good chance I will be found guilty. The evidence was handled properly as far as he can see and documented well by the police. It is going to be tough."

"You will do fine. How can a jury find you guilty of saving a little girl's life against a monster who attacked you?"

"They can because lawyers and judges tell them what they can listen to and how they are supposed to receive information. It is a big chess game."

"Sad, Mom, and I thought my career was pathetic about such conjectures."

"Is that one of them there college words?"

"No, I am creating my own language so I don't become indoctrinated by someone else's."

"Smart girl!" Vickie looks around and says, "Let me preach some things to you for a bit. I may not have the chance later."

"Of course, Mom."

"I know you have been somewhat perplexed by your life as a scientist and being raised religious. Let me give you my take on this and it may not be the answer but might help you get to the answer. I have had the benefit of learning a few things from a man named Professor Chan back in my college days. For me there is no conflict between religion and evolution as you cannot have two truths. There is one truth but the facts of it are divided in two camps. As a marketing expert, I know this all too well that people tend to divide themselves, whether it be religion, sports, or friends. You can take a group of likeminded people who are very close in beliefs and put them on an island. A month later there will be at least two villages on that island. It is inherent, instinctual that people divide into groups. You can't have 'an us' without 'a them.' This is why you have religions subdivide over centuries and split off into other religions. People get stagnant with life or traditions and want something new. Someone comes along providing something different that challenges the status quo. In terms of religion in general versus evolution, it really does not have anything to do with God or science. God is God and religion is man's method to understanding him, and science is simply a process to understand nature. Religion and evolution are the mythologies created by the two camps of people, those who believe in God and those who don't. You might say evolution is the religion of atheists. Don't think of it is true therefore the other is not. Religion is about emotion and evolution is about intellect. Just because one covers a separate function in life does not mean the other is wrong. The reality is both are needed because one requires faith and the other skepticism, both are useful. Running them separately though creates miscalculation of the reality of life and what we are about. Instead of these two camps coming up with a theory and then only looking for evidence to support that one theory, they should look at all. Let me give you an example of what I am talking about. Who invented the theory of the big bang?"

"Well, scientists did."

"Yes and no. It was created by a physicist but he was also a Catholic priest. It was his theory that all things were created at one time, in one place by a Creator. Scientists at the time found the theory to be ridiculous and even Einstein said it was implausible. The Pope canonized it as the proof of a Creator. Well, the theory did not go anywhere that much till some scientists adopted it as their theory of the proof that things exploded and that is why the universe is expanding. It now became an evolutionary belief to which religious people discounted it as ridiculous themselves. So you see, the theory did not change in structure, only in the camps it was in. The lesson is that as divided people, we only have half the story and as long as theories change, it proves it was wrong to begin with."

"How can we get to an ultimate truth being divided like that?"

"It is nature why we divide, maybe it is God's wisdom to make us do that. Because if we were united in one belief and cause, what if it was wrong? The division serves to question things and challenge everything. But if we do develop understandings in different camps and bring it together with an open mind, we might find answers much bigger than our questions could ever hope to be. My advice to you is treat religion as an emotion and science as your intellect. Keep them balanced, use them both equally and you will be all right. That is my motherly sermon that I never had a chance to give you as a young girl."

"Wow, that is deep and confusing at the same time. It will take me some time to process it."

"It will take you your whole life, trust me. I had one benefit of being mentored by some great people and one in a strange way by the name of Violet."

They both pause in silence, then Veronica asks, "Mom, let me ask you something very personal."

"Sure, sweetie."

"Would you have kept me as a baby if your parents had not taken me from you?"

"It was so hard back then, I was young, scared, the events of what happened to my dad and how you came to be, it all just cooked my mind to nothing. There was no reasoning out what I should or could do. But emotionally I could not give you up."

"So maybe that is why God gave us two divided sides to our minds, where your intellect was failing you, the emotion kept you wanting me. I think I understand what you are trying to convey."

"Exactly."

"Thank you for everything you have done for me."

"You were the one thing I did right in life, the circumstances of how it happened doesn't matter. They really don't."

"We are going to beat this court thing."

"That sounds like faith rather than scientific."

"It is faith that I believe you will win and that is driving my intellect to find ways to make it happen."

Vickie smiles and they cuddle together pondering the future.

The Trials of V

Court day for Vickie as she is joined by numerous coworkers, friends, and family all wearing red ribbons upside down to form the V sign. She has already been through jury selections as this is her first day of the actual trial. The prosecutor is Harold Black, a young, aggressive assistant district attorney hoping to make a big splash in this case.

Black begins his allegations. "Your honor, members of the jury, this is going to be a very emotional trial. The accused, Vickie Newsome, seems like a nice lady, but in contrast she is highly trained in the martial arts and in fact has taught in several schools earning high levels of skill in her art. I will show how she used her advanced training to beat a man to death. I will prove that she knew where this man lived, broke into his house, and mercilessly beat him to death. This man never had a chance. The evidence will prove that not only did she do this act of murder, but with her skill could have simply subdued him easily. Instead, she went to his home with the full intention of killing him. The evidence will show that this is not the only man that she has ever done this too. She has beaten in the same way another man but he survived to tell us about it. In this case, you will learn that her hair was found on the murder weapon and even the young child present at the victim's home spoke to the accused as she left her there tied up for the police to find. This further proves that she knew her guilt and tried to run from it. Thank you, ladies and gentlemen."

Guy Jones steps up to speak. "My client, Vickie Newsome, is an executive of a well-respected company and has maintained a good work life that has brought her to be trusted to run a multimillion-dollar company. A company that even today believes in her innocence and backs her 100 percent through this trial. It is true she has advanced martial art training. Has she had to use it to defend herself in the past? Absolutely. She has had good reason to. She is a victim of rape as a young lady but managed to pick up the pieces of her life together, become successful in work, and even reunite with her daughter who was taken from her long ago. Everyone she has come in contact with benefited from her wisdom and charity. How could someone of this character with all the people even here in court in support of her have done such a heinous crime? Thank you."

Guy sits down as the prosecution calls their first witness.

"Tanya Stamp, please take the stand."

Tanya rises and is sworn in as Black begins his questioning. "Mrs. Stamp, you were the child who was kidnapped by the murder victim."

"If you can call him a victim, he was a predator."

"Quite true, he was a predator, but that does not give Miss Newsome the right to kill him."

Guy stands up and says, "Objection, leading the witness."

The judge says, "Sustained."

Black continued, "Mrs. Stamp, you were tied up and held in the victim's bedroom and what did you hear prior to his death?"

Tanya replies, "I heard him say you can't come in here and that is when I tried to yell through my gag. I heard the bedroom door open and my kidnapper say he was going to kill whoever was there."

"Careful, Mrs. Stamp, whoever, really?"

"I had no idea who was there, all I heard was my kidnapper and fighting."

"But the person who killed the kidnapper came to the bedroom and told you who it was."

"They said they were Vickie in a female voice but I could not be sure it was her."

"Who else could it be? Who would claim to be Vickie specifically if they were not?"

"I don't know, like I said, I was gagged and tied up."

"No further questions."

Guy walks over confidently and asks, "Tanya, was Vickie involved with you in self-defense and scouting?"

"Yes, she was."

"Would you recognize her voice easily back at that time?"

"Absolutely."

"But you are not sure if that was her in that predator's bedroom?"

"Not sure it was her."

"So it could have been your mind hoping it was her since she was a role model, correct?"

"Yes. I prayed she would come to rescue me." Tanya starts crying. "I was so scared, so scared!"

Guy finishes, "No further questions."

The prosecution calls their next witness. "John Patterson, please take the stand." John comes into the courtroom being directed by a bailiff outside.

Vickie looks, covers her face as if she is fixing her hair, and whispers to Guy, "Shit."

Guy asks, "What does he know?"

"Everything."

John is sworn in as he sits in the witness chair and the prosecution begins.

"Mr. Patterson, you are acquainted with Miss Newsome?"

"I am. We dated in college and recently too."

"Really? And why the break up between you two after college?"

"I have a drinking problem and she had left me." John keeps looking at Vickie as this is the first time Vickie has appeared to worry. The prosecutor looks at Vickie as he knows this is going to work for him.

"Mr. Patterson, did Miss Newsome ever show violence towards you?"

"Yes, she has several times."

"Could you elaborate on when and how she was violent towards you?"

"In college, I kind of forced myself on her and she struck me with her fist. The second time was after my wreck and recovered from the hospital. She had helped me and was by my side but she picked up a stick and threatened to beat me with it if I did not get my life straight."

Black picks up the murder weapon which is a stick and asks, "You mean a stick like this one?"

"Yes just like that one."

"No further questions."

Guy stands up and ponders a bit. "Mr. Patterson, is it true you were in love with Vickie?"

"I am in love with her."

"So it is safe to assume you are a scorned lover who wants to get back at my client?"

"Objection, Mr. Patterson is not on trial here," Black exclaims.

The judge says, "Sustained."

Guy continues, "Mr. Patterson, the prosecution asserts that my client was violent toward you to equate guilt of the crime she is accused of committing. But do you feel that maybe she was just upset in the fact you had killed her friend in a drunken car accident and grabbed something nearby?"

"I can never bring back our friend from that day." John looks over at Vickie as she is visibly emotional. "I loved her and would do anything for her, but my drinking and my jealousy simply consumes me. I was obsessed with her and had things I took from her just to have something of hers in my possession. But she would not have anything to do with me after getting me a job, mainly because I could not stop drinking. She would fix me for a while but I would keep leaning on her to fix me again. She simply stopped helping me and I grew angry and hated her. But I could not stop thinking about her."

Vickie's head hangs down hearing his words.

John says, "That is why I framed her for the murder I did."

Vickie slowly looks up as the courtroom gasps and Black looks perplexed at his star witness.

Guy says, "Excuse me, could you repeat that?"

"I followed Vickie that day and after she met with Tim she went out apparently looking for Tanya. I saw her approach the victim's house and confront him. I don't know what was said, I was too far away but she left. She seemed convinced he was the predator and left. I saw my opportunity to get back at her since she had been there and got into a small scuffle with the man before he was forced out. I came in through an open window and grabbed that stick on that table and beat that man to death. I then heard Tanya crying in the other room and talked in the best way I could to impersonate Vickie to tell Tanya it was Vickie and help is coming. I planted her hair on the weapon and left. I hated myself for what I did. I love you, Vickie, and I am sorry I did this to you!"

The courtroom is completely quiet as everyone is looking at everyone else.

"No further questions."

Prosecution is shuffling through papers and talking to paralegals as the judge asks, "Mr. Black, any further questions?"

Black ignores the judge and the judge asks again more firmly. Black stands up and says, "Your honor, in light of what was just given in the testimony of Mr. Patterson, we would like to drop the charges and move to have Mr. Patterson arrested for the murder."

The judge agrees and dismisses the case against Vickie as police handcuff John. John just stares at Vickie as she is crying. Family and friends are all hugging each other and Vickie as the court clears.

I Am Not Your Father But Your Lover

Several weeks pass and John's trial accepts his confession of guilt and sentences him to twenty-five years in prison. After being processed to prison, Vickie visits John.

"John, why did you do that for me?"

"I have prostate cancer and have had it for a while. It is why I started drinking again. Did not seem to be a point to it anymore. They can operate but it's not likely it will help. I planned to testify against you as I was angry but sitting there and hearing Tanya's testimony broke me up and I had to leave the courtroom till I was called. I did some thinking and that you helped everyone, you saved that girl, and you were going to fry for that? No. I am dying so it does not matter. They can have their sacrifice on the judicial altar. It was the only gift I could give you that I knew you would not refuse."

Vickie's eyes have tears rolling down as she says, "I love you, John, always have." She uncovers her hand and has the engagement ring John gave her earlier. "You mailed this to me to be delivered after that day of the trial. Why, if you were so angry with me?"

"I knew the trial would go for weeks and you would get it. It was my thumbs up at you but now I am glad I sent it before I was arrested. Remember me, will you?"

"Always. You will always be the love of my life."

John smiles as Vickie kisses the ring and leaves. A few months pass by and John dies from his cancer. Vickie gives him a nice burial site. The headstone has an engraving of the V ribbon from her trial also that reads, "A dear friend that gave all." Once a month she places a red rose on his grave.

My Brother's Keep Her

A year has passed since Vickie's trial and Tanya has a young baby boy by the name of Brian. He is a cute little boy and funny as it is irresistible for people to want to hold him. Life seems to have gotten back to normal for everyone. Tim is still working as principal and Tanya and Sean are doing well in their business. Veronica has been working on a special project involving a new type of telescope. Vickie is having lunch with her old lawyer Guy to discuss old times.

"How are you doing, Vickie?"

"Life is good. How is the legal biz?"

"It is always interesting. Working on a case right now where a man is accused of murder yet he claims his twin brother actually did the crime."

"You believe him?"

"I always believe my clients, it is my job."

"So would that be double jeopardy?"

"You are funny. I wanted to share something. I am teaching a bit now to student lawyers and one of my students was looking up your old case for her paper. She came up with something the prosecution had that never came up in court for obvious reasons. When I looked at it, I had to verify it was true." Guy hands the report to Vickie and she reads.

Vickie asks, "This is accurate?"

"One hundred percent."

"Oh my God, I need to tell Tim this. How could he not know?"

"Maybe he does, but it is not what it looks like."

"Can I keep this?"

"Of course, I brought that for you."

They finish their dinner and Vickie calls Tim to meet him privately. Tim goes to his old park and sits by Vickie.

Tim asks, "So what is so important we need to meet?"

"Tim, we are good friends, right, and you know I would not hurt you."

"I know."

"Tim, your wife Stacie is related to Zane, the pedophile who kidnapped Tanya."

Tim laughs. "What? Is this funny day? They have the same last name but they are not related. She told me she had no siblings."

"No, Tim, I had lunch with Guy, the lawyer, and he brought a file one of his law students discovered. It was in the prosecutions files during my trial. It never got presented to my lawyer because they just discovered it. Here, look."

Tim looks at the report earnestly. "This can't be true."

"Ask Stacie."

"All right, I will, but you will find this to be wrong."

"Did you ever meet her family or see anything about them? I don't remember them being at your wedding."

Tim looks puzzled. "She said that they did not approve of her remarrying, very religious."

"You want me to be with you when you ask her?"

"No, no, that is not necessary. I can handle it no matter what."

"Okay, but I will be waiting by my phone in case."

"Thanks, Vickie."

They leave as Tim makes the long trip back home and as he opens the door Stacie is reading a book.

Stacie asks, "Hey, Timmy, how was Vickie?"

"She is fine, just had some things on her mind."

"Hope it is all okay."

"Actually, I have a question to ask you about your family."

Stacie has a deadpan look as she slowly lowers her book. "Yes, Tim."

"Is the guy who kidnapped Tanya related to you, Zane?"

Stacie closes her book and lays it across her chest with her arms folded. "Yes, he was my brother."

"Why did you not tell me? It could not just be coincidence we got together?"

"Tim, I was divorced and lived away when I heard my brother had been killed. When I heard that you were the suspect but was never convicted, I came back to prove you were the murderer. I watched you and took a job at a carnival place that I knew you frequented. I was hoping to find some kind of evidence to put you away. But after a while I realized the brother I loved was a monster and did not deserve my love and effort to avenge his death. I saw that you could not have killed him as much as I believed you did. I settled in and worked at the bookstore till I became manager. I had forgotten about you and focused on my life. That is, till one day you came in and started talking to me. At first I was intrigued because it was my chance to ask you directly about things. The more we dated and the more I got to know you, I fell in love with you and Tanya. I wanted to be a part of your life. When you told me about Vickie and what she did to my brother, I forgave her instantly. My brother was not my family anymore, but you and Tanya were. I wanted to tell you a million times but I hid as much as possible. I did not even invite my family to the wedding, just told them I got hitched in a spur ceremony. I'm sorry, Tim, for keeping it from you. I love you with all my heart."

Tim is staring down at the ground and looks up at a tearful Stacie. "I don't know how I feel about this. It is too much for me right now. I need to go somewhere, a hotel or something, for a while and sort this out."

"No, Tim, this is your house and your family's. I will leave."

Stacie goes upstairs to pack and comes down to tell Tim, "I will come back for more if need be."

Tim nods his head yes as she slowly walks to the door. Stacie says, "You know, Vickie did the right thing for Tanya, she had no choice but to do what she did."

Tim is tearful as he nods yes and Stacie goes to her car. Tim just stares as she leaves to where he knows not. He sits down and calls Tanya to convey the news. The next evening Tanya comes over to visit her dad.

Tanya says, "Dad, I am absolutely blown away by Stacie and everything."

"I don't know how to feel about this. I can't believe I brought this woman into our lives without knowing who she really was."

"It is not your fault, Dad, it just happened. Do you believe her?"

"My heart does because if her intentions were not honorable she would have done something destructive by now."

"True, I think she is honest about it despite hiding who she really was. Maybe she felt you would end your relationship with her if she told you."

"I just can't have you hurt anymore and this woman represents the biggest hurt in your life."

"I totally get that, Dad, but I am not a child anymore and what happened was long ago. It also was not Stacie who did it but her brother. True, I will think about that man when I see Stacie now, but you know what, I made peace with what happened long ago. I don't want you to throw away your life just because you are worried about me."

"Thank you, Tanya, but I am a father first to you."

"Dad, you are doing your job and doing it well. I am grown with kids of my own now. Please live your life."

"I understand, just give me some time to think about it."

"Sure, Dad. Are you going to be okay?"

"I am fine. Love you, dear."

"Love you too, Dad."

Tanya departs, leaving her dad some more to think about. A few days later, Tanya calls Tim to check on his status.

"Hey, Dad, how are you doing?"

"I am fine. How are you, sweetie, and your hubby and also Victoria and Brian?"

"They are all doing fine, Dad. Brian is a little funny as always, everything has to be perfect or he gets upset."

"Yeah, it is amazing what is important to them at that age."

"How are you and Stacie?"

"Have not talked to her."

"Not good, Dad."

"I think this is just too weird and maybe we should make our separation permanent."

"Really, Dad? You are going to throw away something that has lit you back up?"

"I had about as good a time as someone like me deserves. I am too old to worry about relationships. I have my career and my grandkids to enjoy now."

"At least think about it some more before making big decisions, okay?"

"Okay, sweetie."

They hang up as Tanya calls Stacie at her work and asks if she can come over. Tanya arrives with Victoria as they are greeted by Stacie at her long-stay hotel.

"Oh, lookee here, hi, Victoria." Stacie hugs Victoria and hugs Tanya as they enter the room and sit down to talk. Victoria has a few toys she brought to occupy herself.

Stacie says, "How is your family?"

"Sean and I are doing well at the biz and he is watching Brian sleep, otherwise I would have brought Brian. Brian spends his time stacking blocks in perfect arrangements obsessively. Not sure if I should be worried about that."

"I am sure it is fine, they probably need organization at that age."

Tanya smiles. "I guess so."

"How is your dad?"

"Lost, lost without you."

"Really?"

"He won't admit it as much as he is missing you but it is obvious."

"The only thing that is obvious to me is that I should have been honest up front. That way he could have left me then."

"I know you are a good person and not responsible for what your brother did. I have no hard feelings toward you. In fact, I admire your integrity for choosing right over family."

"It seems what my brother did is costing me two marriages. I have no illusion, there is no way things can be the same after what your dad knows about me. I don't know why I was so stupid to think I could keep such a thing from him. I just wanted to be with him so much."

"Give it some time, he will come around. I know my dad."

"I don't think so. I am looking for an apartment and then that will be that."

"Dad really misses you, I just think you need to give him some time."

Stacie gets up and pulls an envelope out of her purse and hands it to Tanya, saying, "It is too late, Tanya."

Tanya pulls the papers out to reveal that her dad has served Stacie with divorce papers.

Stacie says, "You see, it is over. I just have not had the bravery to sign them yet." Stacie grabs the papers and gets a pen. “Can you give these to your dad the next time you see him?”

Tanya is bewildered and speechless as Stacie begins to sign. Stacie stops for a moment. “You know, the time I got with Tim was the best time of my life.”

Stacie signs the papers and puts them in the envelope to give Tanya. Tanya slowly grabs it and places the papers in her purse.

“I’m sorry.”

Stacie says, “Don’t be, it just was not meant to be.”

In a state of being stunned, Tanya tells Victoria to grab her toys as Stacie gives them all a final hug. Stacie waves good-bye as they leave. Tanya drives over to her dad’s house and Tim answers the door as Victoria is waiting in the car.

“Hi, Tanya, what’s up?”

Tanya throws the divorce papers at her dad and says, “Here you go, Dad, just throw away a woman who was the best thing to happen to you since Mom. I just got these from her and it was nice that you waited to do anything.”

“Honey, it was not going to work out.”

“No, Dad, you were not going to forgive yourself, were you? You know what, Dad, when you divorce, it is not just one person you divorce, it is their family too. Stacie is going to lose all of us because you can’t make peace with yourself.”

“Look, it is more complicated than that.”

"That is crap, Dad, total crap, and you know it. I hope you enjoy being alone for a while because I won't be around either for a while. If you want to visit your grandkids, Stacie will be babysitting them."Tanya leaves as Tim is just bewildered. Just as soon as Tanya's car leaves, Vickie drives up. Tim thinks to himself, *Oh crap*.

Vickie says, "Hey, Timmy, heard you got divorced today."

"You heard that already?"

"Yea, oh these papers them?" Vickie picks up the divorce papers and looks at them. "You know, Tim, you are screwing up bad."

"Yeah right, give me the papers." Vickie tears up the papers and Tim says, "What the hell are you doing?"

"Stopping you from making the biggest mistake of your life."

"Please don't get involved with this one, okay?"

Vickie pushes Tim inside and says, "Guess what? Not going to happen. You are going to reconsider your decision right now."

"Don't bully me in taking Stacie back."

"I'm not going to bully you, I'm going to beat the hell out of you."

"What?"

"You heard me. If you are going to dump this lady, it is going to cost you."

"Now look here, I thought we were friends and past all this violence stuff."

"Violence? You mean like how you violently tossed Stacie's emotions aside and upset your daughter?" Vickie keeps backing Tim up slowly.

Tim says, "Can we just talk?"

"Of course, Tim, I was hoping to scare you a bit." They sit down and Vickie asks, "Why, Tim? She is so good for you."

"It has nothing to do with her brother or what she hid from me. I just keep thinking about the past and all that has happened and just want silence for a moment."

"I see what the issue is. You are haunted by things. Listen, it happens to us all. You know how I deal with it?"

"How?"

"Knitting."

Tim laughs. "What? You knit?"

"That is right, Tim. I can't do martial arts all day long every day, you know. You have to have some moon to your sun sometimes. You know what I mean? Do something opposite to what your nature is. It is called balance, Tim. If you balance yourself, all this crap in your past will go away. You can't lessen the pain sometimes of emotions, but you can develop tools to deal with it better. You know how a baby spills milk and cries? Well, eventually, spilling milk is not such a crying issue anymore. Why? You develop tools to handle it better. The shock of the event is over. You need to forgive yourself completely for what you have done and realize what is good in your life." Vickie gets up, and walks to the door and turns around. "Don't throw Stacie away. You are hurting everyone not because you separated yourself but because you won't be happy, and everyone knows it. That is what upsets Tanya more than anything. Quite frankly, Tim, it upsets me too."

Tim is red in the face as he says, "It is so hard."

"Stop being a stupid bastard, Tim, and get over yourself."

Vickie leaves as Tim goes to the door to watch her drive off. Tim walks up to his room and sits on the side of his bed. The table over in the corner of the bedroom has something fall on the floor. Tim walks over and it is the book he gave his late wife on their first date. Tim looks up and starts to tear up.

The Present Is the Eye of the Compass

Stacie is sitting down watching TV in another boring evening when the door knocks. She answers and Tim is standing there.

Stacie says, "Tim, did you get your papers?"

"I did."

"Is there something I can do for you?"

"I wanted to give you a gift." Tim hands her the book he gave his late wife.

Stacie says, "Tim, I can't take this, it belonged to Lana."

"It belongs to the one I love and that is you. Can you ever forgive me for being such a jerk?"

Stacie hugs him. "I love you, you old goat."

"I love you too, wife."

Stacie looks at Tim. "But the papers—"

"Torn up."

"Oh my, come in."

"How about we pack your stuff and you come with me?"

"You got a deal, mister." They enter and start gathering Stacie's things. Stacie asks, "What changed your mind?"

"I realized you are the best thing to happen to me."

"It will be so nice to go home."

"I made a decision, I am selling that house."

"You can't sell that home, it is your family's."

"It is not *our* home. You are my family and we need to find a home for us, new."

Stacie starts crying and grabs Tim for a hug. "I love you, honey."

They pack and go back to Tim's house and as the weeks pass they find a new home and sell the old house to Tanya and Sean. It is a wonderful dinner as the first dinner in Stacie and Tim's new home is underway with Vickie, Sean, Tanya, and the kids.

Be the Spider

Vickie is conducting one of her weekend self-defense classes to help people not be victims. Stacie walks in the door and sits down in a visitor's chair to watch. Vickie waves to her and points to see if she would like to join, but Stacie waves with no.

Vickie continues, "Class, you need to understand that being a victim is not just circumstance but mentality. Predators look for people not paying attention like walking to your car with your cell phone talking or texting unaware of your surroundings. If you walk to your vehicle, scanning around you once in a while, it is more likely a predator will move on to easier prey. Walk with your keys in between your fingers like little knives sticking out in case you need to strike someone. Don't walk staring at the ground day-dreaming. Some women walk with their hands in their purse holding a can of pepper spray out of view. Always look around and if someone is approaching you and you are near your car, get in and lock the doors. Start your car and drive away. If someone pulls a weapon on you and wants you to get in the car, sit down on the ground. Make them have to carry you, be dead weight. If in an area with other people, scream and run. Try to not get in any car because your chances of survival diminish. Sure they have a knife or a gun and threatening you and you may get stabbed or shot for not complying, but what do you think is going to happen afterward anyway? You need to accept the fact in your mind that you are in serious danger and complying is not going to make it go away. However, if in fact you manage to be in the vehicle with the predator then you need to escape. If a passenger, jump out. If you are driving, drive into a pole or tree. Disable that vehicle before you get too far or speed, drive slightly over the line so it attracts a police officer to pull you over. Don't let them get you to some dirt road and wooded area. You won't be able to outrun them in an open field. Because at that point you are in a fight for your life. The main motive for a predator against women is rape. Obviously kicking his groin is good but there are better things to do. Facing him and he is right in front of you, put your hands on his face as if you want him. Relax him and pull your hands away, make fists and hit him on both sides of the temple. He will drop like a sack of potatoes. Get his weapon immediately and use it on him. You must stop his attack or he will just overpower you and keep coming. You will at most have one chance. Any questions?"

One lady asks, "Should I carry a gun?"

"You need to understand something very well. Unless you shoot thousands of rounds at a range to the point the gun is second nature and your neuromuscular memory is set, a gun can be more dangerous than not having one. It is more likely it will be taken away while you fumble to get it and then if you manage to pull it out in time, you might have a shot or two and chances are you will miss. Most gun shootings miss and are within twenty feet. That is, if you don't hesitate even from worrying about killing this attacker in some moral dilemma. You are better off with a can of pepper spray since we all know how to use a spray can and you are not likely to worry about using it. If it is taken from you, then the attacker does not have a lethal weapon to use. Besides that, even if you have a gun and manage to shoot straight and hit your target, that is no guarantee they are going down. It is not like the movies where you shoot someone and they die instantly. They may not even feel the shot due to shock and keep coming. Your biggest ally is your attitude. If you are attacked you need to get mad dog mean and fight back. Make yourself believe you are the spider and they are the fly. Would you pick up a badger? Of course you would not because the thing would tear you apart. Yet it weighs less and not as strong as you but it is ferocious. That is what it takes, make the attacker want to leave. Now I will show you some self-defense moves that will work."

Vickie shows various techniques as Stacie looks on impressed. After the lessons, Vickie tells Stacie she will be right back as she goes to change clothes. Vickie comes out and she and Stacie go to a nearby coffee shop to talk.

Vickie says, "You interested in lessons?"

"That was awesome, but I wanted to come and thank you about Tim and helping out with our relationship issue."

"You're welcome, I have known Tim for a long time now and I could not let him throw it all away. It is hard for me to say this but I am so sorry about your brother."

"You had no choice in the matter. I lost my brother long before you had to do what you did. You gave him peace and he was too far gone to save. He was a fun loving brother growing up. I don't know what went wrong with him. I left home when he was a teenager and my parents told me he had become withdrawn and a loner. No friends in school and bad grades. He had no ambition to do anything. Maybe if I could have helped him then he could have turned around. But when I came back to seek out Tim, the person I thought had killed him, I did not know to what level my brother had gone to. He had tried to molest a young girl before and became a registered sex offender on probation. He was going to kill Tanya, you know. You saved her and in a way you saved my brother as well as many other victims he would have had."

"When he attacked me I was so enraged seeing Tanya there that I took out everything that had happened to me in life on him. It was different when Tim attacked me long ago. He was pathetic, unsure, even scared. But I just wanted to revenge myself on him and torture him to a point I don't know. I mean, I don't know what I was going to do in the end to him. But he changed. I guess he was not totally lost yet."

"What got into my brother is like any drug that is out there. It consumed him and he was no longer the brother I knew."

"That is correct. Maybe if we treated these people not just as the criminals they are but as addicts, maybe they can be helped."

"I agree, at least before they get to the point my brother got to. Anyway, I wanted you to know there is no issue between us."

"I am glad for that, if you need anything let me know."

"Thank you, Vickie." Stacie leaves as Vickie finishes her drink.

The Syndrome

Tanya had noticed that her son Brian through the age of five appears to have obsessive compulsive disorder and his older sister Victoria exhibits none of the same behaviors. Tanya and Sean have had a difficult time with Brian as they have learned they must detail out instructions for him to do and use the correct wording in conveying their wishes, otherwise he will not perform what was asked. They eventually take Brian to be tested by psychologists and Doctor Pham explains what he has discovered.

"Mr. and Mrs. Stamp, I have reviewed the test results with some other colleagues as well and what your son has is Asperger's Syndrome."

Tanya asks, "Autism?"

"Sort of, it is still something we relatively know little about. It is considered a mild form of autism but really it is in a league of its own. Many famous people have had it, from Thomas Jefferson to Einstein. Typically children who have it are bad in school, difficult for normal parents to cope with, and very methodical."

Sean says, "He is that. If we don't line things out in detail it is like he is lost."

Dr. Pham says, "Exactly. One of the issues is Asperger's is people have a hard time connecting the dots between A and B. However, once they get the logic straight in their head they achieve at great ability. Think of it like we all have a roadmap to our life that tells us where everything is and has the roads to each thing we do. Asperger's map is the same except only the landmarks are there and no roads except what has been previously travelled. If a landmark is moved, we as normal people simply accept the road leads to the new location anyway but with Asperger's, they lose the road completely."

Tanya says, "My poor baby."

Dr. Pham continues, "Yes, it is difficult especially when you can't distinguish between disobedience and they being lost on what to do."

Sean says, "I am ashamed to say I have punished him for not doing what he was supposed to but one day he simply broke down and cried telling me he could not do it. When I questioned him he did not know why. The problem was I simply called the thing I told him to get by the wrong name. He knew what I was talking about but would not get it unless I called it the correct name."

"Right and that is the problem. There are blocks which prohibit them from furthering what they need to do. Most people with Asperger's learn to deal with this like a person who stutters deals with difficult words. They simply reroute themselves around the block with mental gymnastics. They may seem perfectly normal as an adult because they have learned to adjust to the blocks. They often rehearse in their mind what to do in certain situations, even have conversations with people they know or may come across so they can quickly answer with an appropriate response. They generally are very bright and imaginative and can come to solutions very quick if they understand the objective."

Sean says, "Is there something we can do to help progress Brian in this?"

The doctor says, "Yes, I have some reading material that explains the condition in depth and there are some very good books written about Asperger's. You will find it is very common, much more than people realize. One thing you will probably learn is that Brian might take comfort in things like math or science where the logic tends to be more predictable and absolute."

Tanya says, "Thank you, Doctor, for everything!"

Sean says, "Yes, that has taken some weight off my shoulders."

"No problem, remember you are not alone. There are groups to help you understand."

Sean and Tanya leave with a renewed hope that it will be all right.

Vickie calls Tanya. “Hey, how did the results go from Brian’s testing?”

“He has Asperger’s Syndrome, it is a form of autism.”

“I know about it, have an employee with it in our information technology department. He now manages that department. I had a feeling Brian might have something like that because what you told me before of his behavior reminded me of my employee.”

“I have learned a lot about the condition and it has some advantages if properly guided. But it is very difficult at Brian’s age. It is hard for him to understand what normal kids talk about at his age. They tell me that he will likely repeat a grade early on simply to stay at pace.”

“You know what, Tanya, he will be just fine. Our company supports kids with Down syndrome already, I think I am going to fund a little more to support autism foundations as well.”

“That is awesome. We are doing it in our little company now. We have been to some support groups and it has really helped us. How is Veronica doing?”

“She has finished some project and there is a lapse at the moment so she is coming down to visit with me for a while next week.”

"That is nice, hope to see her. I need to run, it is good talking to you."

Vickie says her good-byes as she calls several executives in to discuss expanding their charitable efforts.

Veronica arrives at Vickie's and the two sit down and catch up.

Vickie says, "So, you are out of science gas?"

"Yes, it seems so, funding ran out but we did accomplish what we needed to on our own time."

"So any guys on the horizon for you?"

"Mom, I don't have time for guys, they are such a distraction."

"Don't be such a nerd and start socializing. You know your thirties will blow right past you."

"I know, but I meet so few people in my line of work and spend so much time looking over numbers and grant writing."

"Let me ask you a question, I have been giving something some thought for a while."

"Sure, what is it?"

"What if you had a telescope facility to work in and instead of having to write grants, you spent some time with special needs kids with Down or autism and teaching them science."

"That would be awesome, I have been to several schools and we have given tours to special needs kids before."

"Get me some info on where you could work and do this and let me work out some details with my company."

"You know, it takes a lot of money to fund things like this."

"Well, I now have managing stock in our company and in control now. This is important and we can get mileage out of it with advertising and sponsorships. It would not just be my company shouldering the entire expense. I will make it happen."

"Mom, you are so awesome, but you knew that already, didn't you?"

"Just promise me you will make time to date. Don't let someone as special as you go alone. It is no fun not sharing your life with someone."

"Mom, okay, I promise."

"Very good, and I better approve the dates."

"Mom! Anyway, I am still having a hard time grasping the whole Stacie and her brother thing. What a messed-up world."

"Yes, it was a shock, but I think it turned out for the better for many. So enough of the drama crap, tell me something new and 'sciency.'"

"New and 'sciency,' okay. One of the things I was working was gas analysis of our sun. Well, there is some inconsistencies with how our sun expels gas and even what types for a solar system in our configuration. It was long believed that our planets formed from gas and particles from the sun and to a point that is still probable. However, there is a theory that Mars was closer to the Sun than Earth and there were other planets around Earth's size which are now moons of Jupiter. There possibly was a large planet around where Mars is now and a protostar which is like a star that is not ignited crashed into this large planet causing it to break up into the asteroid belt. Its gravity pulled Mars further out from the Sun past Earth. The protostar broke up into pieces making the gas planets Jupiter, Saturn, Uranus and Neptune. Later Jupiter expelled a planetoid caught in its low orbit and slung it past Earth where it settled upside down and is now called Venus. What do you think of that?"

"As usual, your geekiness has flown over my head. I will have to take your word for it." They both laugh as they settle in for the evening.

And Your Little Dog Too

Tim comes home and Stacie has taken the day off. Stacie says, "Honey, I have a surprise for you."

"Oh, crap, what is it?"

About that time a dog starts barking. Tim says, "Oh, you got a dog finally."

Stacie goes and opens a dog carrier hiding behind the couch and pulls out a beagle puppy.

Tim says, "Why, that is one cute little dog. What should we name it?"

"Sam, after my dog as a kid."

"Was he a beagle?"

"No, he was a big lab."

She puts the dog down and he runs up to Tim as Tim picks up Sam. Sam starts licking his face. He says, "Okay, Sam that is enough. He is adorable."

"You know, Sam is a hound so he will bark loudly when he gets older. But he won't get that big."

"He will be all right."

"He will be our little boy."

"Do you regret not having any kids?"

"A little, but you know what, that is okay. I got to watch Tanya grow up from school age to now and enjoy her kids, so I am fine. Besides, I don't know if I would have been a good parent."

"And I am? You would have been fine."

"Thank you, honey, that was sweet of you." Stacie goes to work the next day at the bookstore and is asked about a good history book by a young man.

"Is this book good about the revolutionary war?"

"It is good and thorough, there is also this one which provides a different perspective than the norm."

"I like looking at things outside the box. Name is Kirk Sampson, by the way."

"Mr. Sampson, nice to meet you."

"Your badge says Stacie and manager."

"Oh yes, sorry, Stacie Jenkins, Mrs. Stacie Jenkins, that is, and I am the manager here." Stacie toggles her wedding ring back and forth in his view.

"Well, Mrs. Jenkins, that is a nice ring, your husband is a lucky man."

"Well, yes, he is, but I am luckier to have him. We have been happily married for a long time now."

"That is really nice, I am still looking out there but like to play the game a little myself before I settle down. Personally I like older women."

"Well, there is no cougar hunting in here, okay?"

"Oh don't worry, I am a gentleman. Very discreet and mature about things. Not after trophies, just a good time, someone mature and clean."

"Clean? What do you mean by that?"

Kirk smiles. "I don't want to catch anything. Kind of careful that way."

"Oh well, I will leave you and your clean self to these books." Stacie walks away and as she works sorting stock she looks over at him as he keeps looking at her and smiling. Stacie keeps appearing to be disinterested but can't help but look once in a while. Kirk buys his books as Stacie purposely avoids him and another clerk helps him. But he leaves and winks at Stacie. She thinks to herself, *Good Lord, Stacie*. She gets home and Tim is playing with Sam.

"How was your day?"

Stacie nervously replies, "It was fine, if you don't mind I need to take a bath real quick."

"Sure, take a load off and relax."

Stacie goes to the bathroom and stares at herself in the mirror, whispering to herself; "What the hell is wrong with you, woman?" She prepares for her bath and has an uneventful evening with Tim and Sam.

A couple of days later, Kirk shows up in the bookstore again. He sees Stacie putting books up and asks, "Stacie, I mean Mrs. Jenkins, how are you?"

Startled, Stacie turns around. "Hi, Mr. Sampson. Back for more revolutionary books?" She turns around and continues stocking.

"Actually, Stacie, I am here for you. I tried to stay away but I had to come back and see you again."

Stacie's head slowly goes down and she turns around. "Look, I am happily married and am in my fifties, you look like a kid to me."

Kirk laughs. "I'm thirty-nine, hardly a kid."

"Well, you look like one to me."

"You don't look like you are in your fifties. Looks pretty sexy for that age."

"I don't know what you think you are going to accomplish here but I am not interested."

"Okay, if that is the way you feel. I thought we had a connection the other day. But you know, I would think if I was you, that being in my fifties I might not get much chance to be with a guy in his prime. Wonder if you will look back on this in ten or fifteen years and wished you took advantage of it."

"Oh my God, I can't believe you said that to me."

"Look, I got you angry, I'm sorry. I respect you but I am very attracted to you. All I am asking is one moment with you. Just one moment to make love to you and we can have what we both want."

"I have been through this before and it did not work out. I think you better go and not come back here."

Stacie turns around as Kirk puts his hand on her shoulder. "Hear me out for thirty seconds."

"I'm listening. Thirty seconds and then you go."

"It did not work out before, you were not with someone smart. If you give me a moment of time with you alone, I will take you places you have never been before. I promise you will live the rest of your life with no regrets. If you say no to me, I will walk out the door and that is the last time you will have this opportunity. Say yes, and you will go home to your husband content with life and feeling something new and young. After, I will leave and never bother you again." He lowers his hand off her shoulder as she looks down.

"All right, one time. Your place after work."

Kirk hands her a piece of paper with his address. "I will be waiting, Stacie." He strokes her hair and leaves. Stacie never turns around but looks at the paper and puts it in her pocket as she slowly whispers, "I never learn."

Kirk is waiting for Stacie and all but given up when there is a knock at his door. He opens and invites Stacie in. As she walks in, she says, "Mr. Sampson, Kirk, you are a very handsome man and very sexy but I can't do this to my husband."

"Stacie, we are having sex, not having you leave your husband."

Stacie looks down as Kirk lifts her chin and starts to kiss her. The passion grows stronger as he walks her into his bedroom.

Driving home, Stacie keeps going around different places to stall as she cries about what she has just done. When she finally manages to get a hold of herself, she goes home.

"Honey, you are done with inventory?"

Stacie walks slowly in as Sam is at her feet barking. "I am tired; I need to get cleaned up and go to bed, okay?"

"Sure, honey, are you okay?"

"Fine, I am fine. Sam, go away."

Tim looks at her funny but shrugs it off and continues reading his book as Stacie goes upstairs. The next morning it is the weekend and Tim has made breakfast.

"Good morning, honey." He reaches to kiss her on the cheek but she has no reaction.

"Good morning," she says.

"Are you all right?"

"I am a little ill today. I'm sorry I am not very hungry. Think I need to just sit and think to myself a while." She goes outside and sits on the porch swing. Tim eats his breakfast and spoils Sam with scraps as he sits and stares at Stacie sitting out there alone. As the week goes by, Stacie is more distant avoiding deep conversations with Tim. Also very to herself at work as well. She begins to feel burning in her groin and sees a doctor privately. The doctor tells her she tested positive for Gonorrhea and gives her antibiotics. She refuses to be close to Tim for weeks as he starts to think he has done something wrong.

One evening, he asks, "Stacie, I have been patient but I need to know, are you okay?"

"I am fine, just going through some changes right now."

Tim is like a light bulb turned on. "Oh, okay, honey. I should have guessed it. I am sorry the change of life has hit you. Is there anything I can do to help you?"

Stacie kisses him. "No, honey, I will be all right. I have been seeing a doctor and it will be okay."

Tim gives her a shoulder rub and she feels somewhat more relaxed that her cover story has worked. Tim walks away when Stacie says, "Tim, I need to tell you something." Tim sits down. Stacie looks around till she finally gets the courage up. "I had a one night stand weeks ago. I wasn't looking for it, someone came in the bookstore and he came in several times and kept working on me. He was in his thirties and made me feel old but would make me feel young. I am so stupid. Told him that I was happily married but he kept sayings things that, I don't know, it just made me feel like it was my last chance at youth. When I met with him and we made love, I really did not even enjoy it. Even physically, it was like nothing. I left crying and feeling like I ruined everything for a moment of lust. It is so hard to explain, I was just plain weak. So it was not a change of life. To make things worse, I ended up getting VD from him and had to take antibiotics to get rid of it. I am clear now and it did not progress to anything worse, thank God. I blew it." Stacie looks up and Tim sits there with a dead pan look. "Say something, Tim, yell at me or something."

A long quiet pause between them as Tim paces around and then sits down. Tim says, "We are getting old and I would be lying if I was not tempted looking at younger ladies. But it seems men are not approached as easily as women are. I don't know what I would do if I was approached by a young lady. So how can I judge you? I like to think I would not because I am happy with you."

"I really tried to dissuade him but he would not let me go. I knew even before we started making love that this was not what I needed."

"What did you need?"

"My youth and a child. What a screwed up way to show it, right?"

Tim gets up and sits next to Stacie. "I think I understand that. I am hurt and it upsets me what you did, but it is not worth throwing what we have away."

Stacie starts crying. "Really?"

"Yes."

"Now I have this hanging over my head."

"Forget about it. It is nothing now. Let's move forward. I love you and forgive you."

"How did I ever deserve you?"

"One of us will fall sometimes, but if we truly love each other, the other will pick us up."

"You can count on me for sure."

They hug and kiss each other but Stacie has a concerned look on her face.

Tim asks, "What is wrong?"

"This guy, his name is Kirk and he has come back in the store. I told him about the infection he gave me and he laughed it off and tried to pick me up again. He comes in on Tuesdays and Thursdays almost like clockwork. What am I going to do?"

"Let me work on it and we will figure out something."

It is Thursday at the bookstore and Stacie is working behind the counter when Kirk comes in smiling and winking at her. Stacie just shakes her head and continues working. Kirk browses the books as he keeps looking over and smiling at Stacie. Suddenly a voice behind him asks, "Is that a good book?"

Kirk turns around and says, "I think it might, name is Kirk."

"Name is Vickie, nice to meet you."

"You are new to this place."

"My first time, a virgin, if you will, ha-ha."

Kirk smiles. "Well then, you need a guide, someone with experience in such things to help you along. I am just that kind of gentleman to educate you."

Vickie smiles. She is wearing a red dress and red lipstick. "I am shy though and scared of new things. Are you discreet about your teaching?"

"Yes, ma'am, I am. I must say you are a beautiful flower alone in the field."

"Stop it, you are embarrassing me. I am not used to someone giving me attention."

"You not getting attention? I find that hard to believe. Such a beautiful blonde and well-built lady. Hmmm, I refuse to believe that."

"Well, I don't get out much. I just spend my time writing code on computers all day. Sometimes I take a break and look at men on the internet. That seems to be the only action I get."

Kirk stands straight up and clears his throat. "Well, I think I can certainly help you in this area. You won't need that internet again, I promise."

Vickie looks around sheepishly and whispers, "Do you live close by here?"

Kirk smiles and whispers back, "Just around the corner."

Vickie looks behind her, rubbing her hands down the sides of her dress up and down and then looks at Kirk and nods yes.

Kirk motions his head to the right and says, "Come on."

Vickie follows behind him as Stacie looks up at Vickie and smiles. Vickie winks and smiles back as Stacie goes back to writing, smiling, trying not to laugh. Kirk and Vickie walk outside and Sean walks up.

"Vickie! Hey, you look great."

Vickie turns to Kirk. "Kirk, this is my friend Sean. Sean, my new friend, Kirk." Both men shake hands and greet each other. "I forgot something I needed inside, be right back, okay?"

Kirk says, "Sure."

Vickie walks in and Sean asks, "So you and Vickie have something going?"

"She seems like a nice lady, we met a couple of times."

Sean has a smirk on his face listening to the lies. "You know, I have known her for years even before the operation."

Kirk turns quickly. "Operation?"

"Surely she told you she used to be a man? Look at her build. Lots of procedures and hormone therapy to get her to that point. She just has the final one left, you know, to get rid of the old pointer."

"What?"

"I'm sorry, I thought you knew but she would have told you soon enough. She is honest and shy about things. This does not bother you, does it? I mean, I don't think anyone would blame you with someone as good looking as her."

"No, she is fine. We are just social friends anyway."

"Oh, okay. Well, I am going to run off, tell her I said bye, would you?"

"Sure."

Sean turns to leave and then turns back and says to Kirk, "Oh by the way I am just kidding about her having a sex change. It was a mean joke, she is a real woman."

Kirk gives a half smile and nods yes as Sean leaves. Kirk has a disturbed look on his face as Vickie returns.

Vickie says, "Okay, that is done."

"Fine, good. Can I ask you a question?" Kirk asks

"Sure, anything, I am all yours."

"You ever have, I mean, do you take hormones for anything?"

"Oh yes, I am an older woman and have to."

Kirk slowly turns away, pondering.

Vickie asks, "Are you okay? It is because I am old, right?"

"No, that is okay. You are fine, just curious about something. You are a woman right?"

"Of course I am a woman."

Kirk laughs a bit. "I mean, have you ever been a man?"

Vickie looks upset. "What did Sean tell you?"

"He said, I mean he indicated, would you please stop that for a moment." Vickie stops rubbing his arm as Kirk continues, "Thank you. He said you used to be a man and had an operation and hormone therapy."

Vickie laughs. "That is silly, I am a woman. But I must warn you that I am having some female issues right now downstairs, you know what I mean? So when we go back to your place I need to stay fairly clothed down there. But we can do everything else."

"I see, but I must insist that I at least see it, you know, so I can get in the mood, otherwise it is hard for me to perform."

"Are you worried if the carpet matches the drapes because I assure you they do."

Kirk laughs a bit. "No, I am sure they do, just like to see for sure though."

"Sorry, not on the first date, I would really like you to get to know me better first before I let you in on the big surprise."

Kirk starts feeling very uncomfortable. "Why don't you just tell me the surprise now?"

Kirk does not want to give up on Vickie's beauty but is visibly disturbed as Vickie replies, "Oh no, it will have to wait. Otherwise you won't call me back." Vickie puts her finger on his lips.

"Oh, believe me, if things check out on the first date, I will call you back."

"I don't think so, I know guys. You say that but then you leave and never call back."

"Look, maybe we should call it off because I have some things I need to get to."

"Well, okay, if that is how you feel, fine. I guess I need to go back in the store and apologize to Stacie."

"Apologize to Stacie, for what?"

"We are married, don't you know? I used to be her husband till the operations started now I am her wife. Okay, you happy, you got it out of me. I was hoping you and I would hook up because I prefer men now. Especially after the gonorrhea I got from Stacie weeks ago."

Kirk has a very disturbed and puzzled face.

Vickie continues, "You know, I can't judge her though because I gave her much worse than that. That is why I did not want you to mess with my lower parts at least till we figure out what Stacie and I have. That and of course the pointer, which is yet to come off in future operations. That is, if the doctor will clear this up what we have."

"I need to leave, sorry." Kirk runs to his car and starts it as he looks at Vickie. Vickie gives him a brokenhearted puppy dog look as he drives off. Sean comes back over to Vickie and Stacie walks out to meet them. Vickie turns around to them. "I guess he was itching to go." They all laugh as Kirk is driving to the nearest doctor to get checked out.

Stacie returns home and Tim asks, "Well, how was your day?"

Stacie laughs. "Oh my God, I am still laughing. Vickie really did a number on that Kirk guy." Stacie details the encounter with Kirk and Vickie as Tim smirks and laughs once in a while.

Tim says, "She is good."

"Yes, she is. Thank you for cleaning up my mess."

"No problem, honey." They sit down for a nice evening.

The next week Tuesday at the bookstore Stacie is shelving some new books when she turns around and Kirk is standing next to her with an angry look.

"Mr. Sampson, can I help you?"

He stares for a bit as Stacie looks around and back at him. "Nice little scam your friends played on me. I got checked out and there is nothing wrong with me. I realize you wanted to get rid of me but I don't like being played. I will be back Thursday, have Vickie meet me here, usual time. Okay?"

"Look, it was all in fun and no harm done, okay?"

"Have her show up or I keep bothering you instead."

Kirk leaves as Stacie calls Vickie at work. "Vickie, we have a problem." Stacie tells Vickie what has just transpired.

Vickie responds, "I will be there. Don't worry."

Thursday rolls around and Stacie and Vickie are in the middle of the store talking when Kirk shows up and walks over to them. Kirk just stares at Vickie as Vickie asks Stacie to give them a minute. Stacie leaves, and Kirk says, "Pretty funny making me look like a fool."

"Wasn't a hard stretch for you."

"Why don't we begin again on this? How about a date, my place right now."

"Might hurt, little boy, I like it rough."

"I can take it."

"Can you? Tell you what, I volunteer at the martial arts place not far from here, how about you get some lessons, on the house."

"No, thank you. More of a chess player myself."

"I see. Well, your move first then."

"Got to warn you, I never lose."

Vickie smiles. "All right."

Kirk stares at Vickie as he turns and leaves. Stacie walks up to Vickie and asks, "You okay?"

"Yeah, I am fine."

"I am so sorry I got you into this."

Vickie smiles at Stacie and starts to walk away; "Don't worry, I live for this."

The next day at work, Vickie gets delivered a beautiful bouquet of flowers with a balloon that is a condom blown up. Card in the flowers reads "Sorry for your loss." One of Vickie's executives asks, "Hey, Vic, I see someone likes you or did I miss a big occasion?"

"No, it is just my new friend that likes to embarrass me."

The exec starts walking away, saying, "Embarrass you, he has a lot to learn."

Vickie whispers to herself, "He will."

Kirk comes home to his apartment and on the doorstep is a bouquet of roses in box with red vase sitting next to it and a card stuck in the vase's neck. He reads the card: "Itching to repay you for the gift." Kirk brings it all inside and fills the vase with water to put the roses and extra floral greenery. Kirk says to himself, "At least she saved me some money for tonight." Kirk gets ready for his date and goes out to meet this new person he has just picked up. He arrives at her apartment and gives her the roses. She smells them and tells him she loves them. They leave to eat at a nice place and as the conversation is getting romantic they both start itching. As the evening goes on it gets worse and worse till finally they seem to be breaking out in a rash. Kirk takes his date home and goes to his apartment to find he is broke out on his arms. He starts putting some cream on the rash which seems to relieve it somewhat. A little later his date calls and tells him; "You bastard, you think this is funny? Putting poison ivy in my flowers. I am breaking out all over my face and hands. Don't call me again!"

She hangs up and Kirk is furious. He drives down to the store to get poison ivy cream.

Vickie arrives home a couple of days later to find a book leaning against her door. She looks around and goes inside, leaving the book out there. She comes back with rubber gloves and picks the book up and takes it to her backyard patio. She then gets a long stick and starts opening the book and everything seems normal but she does not trust it. She calls everyone she knows if they delivered a book to her but no one knew about it. Vickie simply places it in the trash outside. Late that night she hears cats meowing outside and going crazy. Running to the commotion outside the cats have knocked her trash can over and were shredding the book apart. Apparently parts of it were soaked in cat nip. Vickie takes the book inside to bag it up and says to herself, "Clever but weak." The next morning, she notices dead spot of grass in her yard. Everywhere a dead spot was there is a broken balloon. Vickie thinks to herself, *Little bastard threw water balloons of weed kill in my yard to get me in trouble with our HOA.* Vickie calls her lawn service to fix the issue. The next day, Kirk is scooping up various nuts out of the health store bins when Vickie walks up.

"Hey, Kirk, nice to see you again."

"Vickie, the grass greener on the other side?"

"Funny, I was just thinking that. Getting some nuts for home?"

"Office, I like to promote good health."

"How noble of you."

"You should get some. Help keep you sharp."

"I may but some of these give me an awful rash."

Kirk laughs. "Yea, roses do me. Well, see you later."

Vickie smiles as she gets a bag of cacao beans which look much like almonds. While Kirk is distracted she manages to swap his almonds with the cacao beans. Kirk is loading up his bags as he looks over at Vickie eating a bag of almonds and she waves. Kirk waves back and says to himself, "Whatever." Kirk arrives at work and starts putting the nuts in a large bowl and places it in the center of the conference table. Later that afternoon there is a staff meeting and the president of the company thanks Kirk for getting the nuts. Everyone is enjoying them till finally one person chews a cacao bean and starts to gag a bit. He leave the room and everyone continues the meeting. Another person grabs a cacao bean and starts to spit it in the trash. They tell everyone that some of those nuts must be bad, that was the most awful thing they have ever eaten.

Kirk looks at the bowl and asks which one they just ate. The coworker points to the almond looking one as Kirk picks one up and says, "That is not an almond, that is a cacao bean." Someone asks what that is, and Kirk replies, "It is what they eventually make chocolate out of but in their pure form, they are very nasty tasting." Then he remembers Vickie eating almonds in the parking and says, "Vickie." The president asks if they can continue with the meeting and get rid of the nuts. Kirk sits through the meeting, embarrassed and plotting his next revenge.

A week seems to have passed by with no incidents so Vickie gets up on Saturday and goes out to get her paper when she notices neighbors staring at her lawn. She is thinking, *What now?* She looks at her lawn and there are a couple of dozen lawn gnomes painted to look like Nazis with a little Hitler in front. She gets a trash bag and gathers them up, telling her neighbors she has been pranked by college kids. Vickie thinks to herself, *That takes things up to a new level.*

Kirk gets a call at home one evening from his mom and dad and his mom asks, "Son, there was a woman here looking for you, said you were the father of her baby."

"Mom, was she blonde and strong looking?"

"She was blonde and very pregnant, said she was Vickie. Said you refused to marry her and she does not know what to do about her unborn child."

"Mom, that woman is a practical joker friend of mine who is taking the jokes too far. She is not pregnant and too old to get pregnant, I bet."

"Looked real to me. She looked like she was about to go into labor at one point and had a hard time getting up."

"Mom, it is a sick joke. Don't worry about it, I will tell her to leave you guys alone."

"Your dad wants to talk to you."

His dad says, "Son, if you are in trouble we are here to help."

"Dad, it is a joke. She is not pregnant."

"Son, you need to take responsibility for this girl. Especially since she got pregnant from you paying for sex from her. Don't you have the sense to use a condom?"

Kirk gets angrier. "Dad, she is not pregnant and she is not a prostitute. Look I will talk to you guys later." Kirk hangs up and clenches his fist pacing around. Later Vickie gets a knock on the door and it is Kirk.

"Kirk, old friend, got your gnomes in a trash sack if you want them back."

"Can I come in for a bit?"

Vickie invites him in and Kirk says, "Look, this has all gone far enough with my parents."

"You do have nice parents, so sympathetic. They were offering to give me money from their savings, you know, for our baby."

"That's not funny. I am done with this now. You crossed the line with my parents."

"You crossed the line when you slept with my friend's wife."

Kirk turns around rubbing his face. "You're right. That was wrong, but most older women have needs too and what does it hurt giving them a little pleasure."

"Nothing, unless they are in a committed relationship. You realize you could have ended a marriage. That lady was vulnerable and you took advantage. What happens if someday you have a wife and some young punk has her?"

"Look, I get it, it was bad. Married women have some advantages because they have someone to go back to and don't cling on you."

"That is a good theory, except you can't have any relationship without someone clinging to you. Even if they are married, they will feel loss. Maybe not the loss of losing someone like you but the loss of trust and respect for themselves. You just don't get it, do you?"

Kirk intently stares as Vickie says, "We are done, right? No more me, and no more Stacie. I can't stop you from other women. I just hope you mature someday."

"It is over, you and Stacie won't see me again."

Kirk walks to the door and turns a bit. "You know, I am not a bad person really. Just having fun among consenting adults."

"Bad is a relative statement. When you step over the line, it is no longer bad but normal. Eventually you are so far away from what real normal is, you don't even remember where you were."

Kirk looks at Vickie and walks out.

Mutiny on the County

Tim arrives for another typical day at work in school. Disciplinary issues with students, budget issues, parents upset over one issue or another, teachers fed up with students and the system. All in a day's work, it seems, running a public school. But this day, Tim gets a call from an anonymous student that tells him Billy Somergate, a sophomore, has brought a gun to school. Larger school systems have police to investigate tips but in a small town and low population county, these resources are a luxury. Tim is more concerned with making sure low-income students get to eat in the subsidy program than turning school into a prison system. Tim goes to Billy's class and excuses himself for the interruption.

"Susan, John, Billy, Doug, please grab your stuff and come as you have been selected for a new project. It will take just a few minutes."

The four grab their books and packs as they follow Tim to his office. Tim is outside his office when he says, "Who wants to be first to know the secret?" He gets no response as the four look at each other but Tim smiles. "You guys are no fun. How about you, Billy? Go in my office and I will tell you the secret first." Billy strolls into Tim's office and sits down. Tim whispers, "You three go back to class. I just need Billy for the moment." The three teenagers shrug their shoulders and leave back to class. Tim tells his administrative person to leave for a while. As she leaves, Tim goes in and sits on the front of his desk in front of Billy. Billy sits in the chair holding his backpack in his lap.

"Hi, Billy."

Billy responds, "Hi, Mr. Jenkins."

"How are you doing, Billy? Things okay at school?"

"Fine."

"Is there any issues with bullying because you know we have zero tolerance of things if someone is bothering you."

"No one is bothering me, Mr. Jenkins."

"Well, you seem a little bothered and you know I am here to help."

Billy looks around and asks, "Where are the other guys?"

"Oh I sent them back because I really wanted to talk to you."

"About what?"

"I am going to level with you. I plan to retire someday and one of the biggest concerns I have is some kid hurting another in this school. I really would hate to go out having that in my career here."

Billy shrugs his shoulders. "What does that have to do with me?"

"Because I believe anyone who has a weapon in school is going to create trouble. They may not intend to use it but may just be scared of something or feel it is cool to have one." Billy clutches his bag a little tighter as Tim continues, "Look, Billy, if there is a problem here or at home, I can help. If you have something dangerous, some other kid might get a hold of it and use it." Billy stares intently at Tim. "I was a teenager once, and I went through some horrible times. I can help, Billy."

"Am I under arrest?"

"No, Billy, just let me have what you have in that bag. We will talk about it."

"I need it."

"For what?"

"I don't want to live anymore."

"Billy, if you plan on using a gun on yourself, you know it is not a sure thing it will kill you. You could be in a coma for years, it could make you mentally retarded, or a vegetable. What about your family? Friends?"

Billy starts tearing up. "I don't have any friends and my father hits me. My mom just watches and does nothing."

"So you took your dad's gun and feel like killing yourself is going to make him feel sorry?"

Billy eyes roll with tears as he says, "Yes."

"Well, it won't. Why does he beat you?"

"He drinks and blames me and my mom for all his problems. He says I am a loser and won't amount to anything."

"You know, that is the alcohol talking."

"Well, it sounds a lot like Dad."

"You are not responsible for his problems, you know that, right? His problems are his own. I could talk to him, maybe get some help for you and your mom. He has no right to beat you."

"It won't make any difference, he has been arrested before but they just let him go and he does it all over again."

"There are services and things that can help. I will help you."

"I don't care anymore."

"You do care or it would not bother you. I need you to trust me. Can you do that for me?"

Billy stops his thousand-yard stare and looks at Tim. "I just wanted to be liked."

"I know, son, everyone does. But you and I and all the rest of the good people on this planet have to stick together and be here for each other. Sometimes life isn't fair and you get stuck with people who are mean. Believe me, I know. But if you really want to get back at your dad, do good in school, go to college, and go further than he ever dreamed he could."

"What about this gun I have?"

"Give me the backpack." Billy looks down and hands Tim the pack. "Good, Billy. It is between you and me. Come with me."

"Where are we going?"

"We are going to your parent's house and then you are coming with me for a while." Billy looks scared. "Trust me."

Billy follows Tim to his car as Tim puts his pack in the trunk. Tim opens the pack to reveal a large caliber handgun and extra clips loaded with bullets. "Billy, if you were going to kill yourself, why did you have these clips?"

"I don't know what I was going to do."

"All right, let's go."

They drive to Billy's house and walk up to the door. Billy's mom answers the door. She says, "Can I help you?"

Tim recognizes the voice. "You called me, didn't you? I am Mr. Jenkins from the school."

She replies, "Yes, I did."

Billy looks confused as they enter the home.

"Is Mr. Somergate here?"

"No, he is at work, why?"

"Billy tells me your husband has been hitting him."

She replies, "That is not true. Billy, have you been telling lies again?"

Tim says, "Well, when a kid brings a gun to school he is crying out about something."

She responds, "You don't understand Billy."

"I think I understand quite enough."

At that moment, a work truck pulls up in the driveway and Billy gets nervous, saying, "Mr. Jenkins, that is my dad. We need to leave."

"It is okay, Billy, I am here."

Billy's dad enters the house and asks, "What is going here?"

Tim answers, "I am Principal Jenkins from the school and I brought Billy home. Apparently he is very frightened of you and spoke of abuse."

Billy's dad says, "Abuse? Are you telling that one again, Billy? Mr. Jenkins, I apologize but he is a compulsive liar."

Billy screams, "I'm not lying!"

Tim says, "Billy, calm down, okay? Mr. Somergate, I have reason to believe that he is abused."

"Find the bruises? Go ahead, look him over."

"I have seen this before and you people cleverly hit them in the head where it is hard to see the bruises."

"Well, look at his head then."

Tim checks Billy's head for lumps or bruises but finds none and responds, "May not be any now but what about you being arrested for abuse?"

Mr. Somergate looks at his wife and they both chuckle while Billy's dad responds, "Mr. Jenkins, I am a deacon in the church. I have never been arrested. Billy is leading you down the primrose path. What you don't know is Billy is bipolar and manic depressive." The dad goes to the kitchen and gets Billy's prescriptions and shows them to Tim. "You see, when he is on his medication, he is just fine."

"Is this true, Billy?" Billy starts laughing and sits in the chair chuckling with a sinister look. Tim looks back at the dad. "Why was the school not notified about this?"

"We wanted him to have the same chances at a normal life as any other."

Tim grows angry. "You realize I have his backpack in my trunk and it has a loaded gun with extra clips."

The dad looks surprised and the mom says, "I called the school and warned them so they would arrest him. I did not expect them to bring him home. He needs help and he is dangerous."

Mr. Somergate says, "He is my son and I love him. Not sending him off to some institution. How could you try to get him arrested?"

"He is taking your gun to school, he is going to hurt someone."

Tim interrupts, "All right, I obviously misjudged this whole situation. We need to call the police, Mr. Somergate."

The dad looks at his son and back at Tim and nods yes. His wife runs over and puts her arms around the dad. Tim looks at Billy with a lot of hurt as Billy stares back with no emotion. Tim calls the police and as they arrive Billy is taken into custody and the weapon confiscated. Tim drives home wiping tears away that he could not help Billy and that things could have gone terribly wrong at school. As he arrives home and goes in to sit down, Sam jumps in his lap and he begins petting and pondering.

Stacie comes in and asks, "You all right, Tim?"

"Yeah, just another day as principal."

Buyouts and Bygones

Vickie calls a meeting with Sean and Tanya to propose a business deal between their companies. Vickie sits down in Sean and Tanya's conference room.

Vickie says, "You probably are wondering why I called this meeting today. How you guys doing over here?"

Sean replies, "Doing well actually, seems markets are loosening up a bit."

Tanya says, "Yes, we have some new client bases that are giving us a 20 percent increase over last year."

Vickie says, "That is good, and for a small marketing company with a handful of employees, you guys have done excellent. Your experience and accomplishment has given a track record that I was hoping for."

"Hoping for what?" Tanya asks.

"As you know, I am managing stock holder of my company now. What would you guys think if my company bought yours and I stepped down as president and put you guys in charge of my company? You would have stock options valued in the amount of your company's purchase, control of my company, higher salary than you have now, and a wider spectrum of clientele."

Tanya replies, "Wow, that is interesting. What are you going to do?"

"I would be the chairman of the board. You guys would manage and run the place, I would just be in the background."

"So you are retiring?" Sean asks.

"Sort of. I will be involved but not actively all the time. It is like a retirement, if you call it that. I want to move on to other things with my time. I earned a law degree online and passed the bar. Not going to be a lawyer but thought about something legal. I have the proposal and figures here about how this merger would happen. Look it over, take your time, and think about it."

Sean says, "Sure, we will look it over. This is big and a lot to take in."

"Of course, there is no rush. The offer is good anytime."

Tanya says, "Thank you for this opportunity, we will consider it carefully."

Vickie gets up and hugs them both. "See you guys later." Vickie leaves as Sean and Tanya discuss the offer and look the figures over. They call for a meeting between their managing staff and invite their corporate lawyer to discuss the offer. After several weeks of meetings, it looks like a solid deal that would give them greater opportunities. Sean and Tanya and kids come over to Tim and Stacie's to discuss what Vickie proposed. Everyone greets and the kids play with Sam.

Sean says, "Vickie has offered to buy out our company and put us in charge of hers. She will take a less active role as a board member and Tanya and I would control things."

Tim says, "Wow, that is a big change. I assume this means more money going from a small company to a larger one."

Tanya says, "It would be a significant change in our income and we would walk in with stock ownership equivalent to our company's value. Matter of fact, it is a little better than our company's value."

Stacie asks, "So what are you guys going to do?"

"We decided we are going to do it," Tanya replies.

"Well, that is fantastic!" Tim exclaims.

"We are excited. It will take a while to transition but it will work out," Sean says.

"How do your employees feel about it?" Stacie asks.

"We had a companywide meeting and discussed what it meant. No one will be laid off and their positions will integrate at a better pay rate in the new company. Plus we offered each one some shares in the new company as well. Some of the executive positions collide with existing positions in the new company, of course, but they were content with number two spots in line for the top spot if available. Basically, everyone was okay with it because it meant more money in their pockets and better benefits. So everyone is a go on it," Tanya explains.

"Well then, I am excited for you and everyone there at your company," Stacie says.

"We also talked about it and I have decided to take a vice president position for a while till Brian starts school and I will step down. I want to focus on our kids more and Brian especially will need more attention going through school. So Sean will be president," Tanya says.

"I think that is excellent and you are doing the best thing for Brian," Tim agrees.

They have a nice dinner and continue with catching up. The next day, Sean and Tanya notify Vickie of their acceptance and within a month their small company is bought out. Vickie takes a long vacation to see Europe and Asia, leaving her company in Sean and Tanya's hands after a few weeks of transition time.

Like We Were Never Apart

Several years have passed and Sean has successfully brought Vickie's company to a new threshold of commerce. Tanya is actively taking care of their kids and coordinating a group effort to help those with autism. Stacie continues to work at the bookstore as Tim is finishing up another year as principal. Veronica is studying efforts in solar astronomy while giving astronomy classes to special needs kids as part of her fund requirement from her mom's company. Vickie has been gone off and on traveling and seeing the world. Vickie drops by Tim and Stacie's for an evening of catching up.

Tim says, "Well, world traveler, did you leave the world the same way you found it?"

Vickie laughs. "For the most part. Summer is coming up you guys need to take a break and see some things."

"We intend to use some generous financial gifts from Tanya and Sean to visit places."

"Honey, you need to tell her your plans," Stacie says.

"Oh yeah, you have been away so much I did not have a chance to tell you. I am retiring after the next school year."

"That is great! What are your plans for retirement?" Vickie asks.

"Well, we are going to try to find a small house on some land near a lake so I can fish."

"I have plenty of hobbies inside, thank you. It won't matter much where we are, just not too hot," Stacie says.

"That sounds nice, have any idea where?" Vickie asks.

"There are some properties to the southwest of us but are a little pricey. We will stumble on something,"Tim says.

"Well, that sounds like a plan. I thought about moving abroad myself. After traveling around, there are some very nice places I would not mind staying at for a while. I have some plans to move into more social responsibilities. I think my talents can be utilized elsewhere."

Stacie says, "I am happy for you. That sounds nice."

Tim says, "I hope you come around once in a while and visit."

Vickie replies, "Oh I will, can't get rid of me that easy. It will be a little while before I embark on this venture anyway." The evening progresses into pleasant conversations of places travelled and things seen.

The summer passes and well into another school year Tim has secured his replacement, Raul Hernandez, as the new principal and is set to retire in a few months. Vickie calls Tim and asks him if he and Stacie would like to see her new place on the weekend. Tim agrees and as the weekend comes up Vickie picks them up to see the new place.

Tim asks, "So you bought another place near here?"

Vickie answers, "Absolutely. You talked about land last year and it got me thinking it would be nice to have a place out in the country."

"Maybe we can be neighbors?"

"Could be."

They arrive and Sean, Tanya, and the kids are there. Vickie gets out of the car. "Glad you guys could see my new place."

Tim and Stacie greet everyone and they start to look around at the open country with a nice lake with a fishing pier on it.

Tim says, "Wow, this place is awe inspiring and so quiet."

Stacie says, "Vickie, you have found the spot."

Tanya and Sean smile as Vickie says, "Yes I knew this was the spot the first time I saw it. Fully stocked lake of fish and quiet. There is only problem with it."

"What is that?" Stacie asks.

"I don't own it, you do."

"What?" Tim exclaims.

"I bought this for you, well, with some help from Sean and Tanya too."

Stacie asks, "What are you talking about?"

Tanya replies, "Dad, Mom, this is all yours."

Tim and Stacie's eyes glaze over the view.

Tim asks, "Which part of it?"

Vickie points and says, "You see those hills over there and the county road on the other side, and to the other side of those trees way out there? All of this."

Tim says, "I can barely see the end of what you are talking about."

"This is all yours and your fishing lake is right in the middle."

Stacie says, "Oh my God, Tim, I don't believe this."

Vickie says, "That is not all."

Tanya says, "We are building you a new house exactly the way you want and fixing this land up with fences, whatever you guys want."

"This is too much, I don't know what to say," Tim says.

"Say thank you, dummy," Vickie jokingly says.

"Thank you."

"Thank you all," Stacie says. She is crying and hugging Tim.

Sean says, "We will take care of the taxes and expenses each year as well. You guys just retire and enjoy it." They all start walking and taking a tour of the area as Tim and Stacie talk about where to put their house up.

Tim officially is retired from being a principal and the school gives him a warm send off by showing old pictures of him and teachers giving him a roast in front of students and parents one evening. He is presented with some awards including a new stadium named after him, as he is given a standing ovation as Stacie, Tanya, Sean, and their kids watch. Vickie is away on her travels otherwise the evening is perfect for Tim. Tim stands up and gives a speech.

"To the parents, thank you for letting me take care of your children and entrusting me with your most valuable asset. To the teachers, thank you for being in the trenches each day and making a difference in these kids' lives. To the staff, thank you for keeping the machine running each day. To the board, thank you for your support of my administration and keeping the doors open. To my family, thank you for I never would have been able to do this job without you. My daughter for her support and believing in a dad that was not perfect by any means. To my wife who stood by me and kept me going day to day. My wonderful grandkids that give me joy each time I see them despite the cookies that mysteriously go missing each time they visit. Finally to

Vickie my good friend that brought me from the brink several times in my life. She could not be here today but she is with me always. Thank you everybody. I am going fishing."

Everyone laughs and stands up again clapping and cheering.

Sunset

THE YEARS ROLL by since Tim retired from being a principal of a large public school. Nowadays, he volunteers at women centers and speaks about how not to be a victim and educates women on the issues of abuse as well as fishing, of course. He is at a large meeting as a guest speaker to a crowd of people at a support meeting for raped and battered women.

"You need to know that what happened to you is not your fault. You did nothing wrong. There is nothing you did to deserve anything that happened to you. I at one time tried to rape a woman. I was in a boring life and a boring marriage and stalked women at a bookstore. I did not understand that the abuse I had as a child from my predator carried on to my adulthood into the need to prey on others. I thought I had put it behind me by ignoring it. I never made peace with the issue and over time I sought to impose my will on another as it had been done to me. I was not mentally sick or diagnosed with a psychological issue. I was troubled and had no guidance in life. But mainly I hated myself and in turn my wife hated what I hid from her which was my emotions. The issue brewed in me like a cancer wanting to eat me alive. Eventually I entertained the emotions in my mind of wanting to hurt someone that I finally tried to carry it out. I followed this lady and when I gained entrance to her home she turned the tables on me and got me down. What I did not know is that she was a rape victim from her teenage years and had well-armed herself physically with self-defense capabilities.

"Needless to say, I was no match for her and she made me pay for it. I thought she was being cruel, but in the end it turned out to be my salvation. She made me and my family face the things we were hiding all those years. The worse thing I did was not sharing myself completely with my wife. If I had nothing bad would have happened. Matter of fact she might be alive today."

Tim pauses and cries for a moment, thinking about her smoking and cancer that maybe she would have not smoked if he would have shared things with her. He continues, "I'm sorry. Please understand bad things hide in the shadows and bringing them out in to the open is the way to keep the issues at bay. We live in a world of isolation thanks to the internet and texting. We are beginning to understand things in short bits of information and context less meanings. We feel safe behind keyboards dropping our inhibitions and manners even. All this does is to serve our base desires and emotional unresolved issues in a new hiding place. Both men and women need to bring out what they feel and not hide behind technology or beliefs that foster the darkness. Don't get me wrong, I know nothing grows in pure water. But we need to not be so politically correct that it stifles communication and honesty however we must be respectful as well as truthful. The biggest thing is to be honest with yourself. This is…"

Tim looks up and there is Vickie in the back of the room smiling. "This is key because if you are not honest with yourself, you will not be honest with others, and you either become prey or victim. Thank you all for hearing me."

Everybody claps and walks up to shake Tim's hand as he watches Vickie leave. He puts his attention back to the people answering their questions and socializing. Later as the meeting disperses he is among the last to leave. Going to his car he sees a rose with a red ribbon tied like a V under his windshield wiper. A note is on the rose that reads:

> Tim, you have become what every man should be.
> Be well and happy the rest of your days.
>
> Love,
> Vickie

He looks over as Vickie is standing by her car. She blows him a kiss and smiles as she leaves. He waves as she drives off and stares at the rose. A feeling of warmth flows over him despite the cold winter night around him. He knows peace and peace has found him.

Court is in session as new case is about to take place in a local courtroom. This court deals with smaller cases not needing a jury, usually domestic situations and smaller crimes of low felony or misdemeanor. The accused is a man that beat his wife, and she finally filed charges on him. The accused is cocky and feels he has the right to do what he did. Where counseling of family has failed to convince him of the error of his ways, now it is the judicial system's turn at bat. He asks his public defender what are his chances. The defender responds, "Well, I really don't know since this judge is new, and I really don't know who they are."

The accused responds, "Great, I hope it is not a woman."

The bailiff bells out in a deep voice loudly, "All rise for the honorable Vickie Newsome!"

Other books and information can be found at:
www.Mazzaroth.net

If you have any comments about this novel please write to:
books@mazzaroth.net

I would love to hear your thoughts.
Thank you for reading my story.

Mike